BIBLE IN POCKET,

GUN IN HAND

Bible in Pocket, Gun in Hand

THE STORY OF

FRONTIER RELIGION

Ross Phares

UNIVERSITY OF NEBRASKA PRESS

LINCOLN

First Bison Book edition: February 1971

CONTENTS

I. Religion Arrives   1

II. The "Brush College" Graduates   10

III. Bible in Pocket, Gun in Hand   25

IV. Emotions in Strong Doses   45

V. Fightin' the Devil   58

VI. "Bad" Preachers and "Badmen" Who Preached   66

VII. Camp Meetings and Great Revivals   76

VIII. Church Discipline before Court Discipline   93

IX. Rivalry among Denominations   118

X. Prayers of the Frontier   130

XI. Scoffers and Troublemakers   144

XII. The Hard Lot of Saddlebag Preachers   155

NOTES   167

BIBLE IN POCKET,

GUN IN HAND

I

RELIGION ARRIVES

The Reverend Freeborn Garrettson reined his horse to an abrupt halt in the deep Delaware woods and listened intently. He heard a man by the roadside ahead singing lustily. The melody lifted the spirit of the minister, riding the lonely outer fringe of his Cypress Swamp Circuit that day in 1779. Here, at last, he thought, was a happy Methodist brother, singing a hymn joyfully as he worked. He hastened toward him.

But on riding closer, he was shocked to discover that the man was singing a profane song. As was the custom of circuit riders, he sought to examine the man on his religious convictions: "Do you know Jesus Christ?" he asked.

"Sir," replied the man, "I do not know where the gentleman lives."

Thinking surely the man had misunderstood him, the minister repeated the question.

"I do not know him," he answered innocently; "he must not live in these parts."[1]

Another circuit rider told of traveling farther out on the frontier and asking a boy by way of testing his knowledge of the Bible: "Who killed Abel?"

The preacher was surprised to hear the lad answer: "I didn't know he was dead. We just moved here last week."

Such was religious ignorance on the American frontier following the colonies' break with England.

After the American Revolution, settlers pushed into the backwoods, reveling in their new-gained freedom, seeking the material opportunities it promised. With land everywhere just for the taking, they spread out thinly. In their rush for political and economic freedom they outraced the established institutions of society—the church, schools, courts of law. Not only ignorance but emotional instability resulted, bringing widespread worldliness, immorality, and infidelity.

Two general misconceptions developed concerning religious influence in the settling of early America: Because life in the new country was relatively simple, temptation weaker, and the people more humble, the erroneous conclusion was drawn that the settlers were more devout. Second, the belief that America was settled mainly by church devotees seeking religious freedom appears to be based more on misinterpreted tradition than statistics. Indications are that the colonists may have been seeking freedom more than religion.

Of the hundred and one immigrants aboard the *Mayflower*, only twelve belonged to the first New England church. Not more than one out of five of the Massachusetts Bay colonists during the early years were members of a church. In 1760 only one New Englander out of eight was a church member. The ratio in the Middle colonies was one to fifteen, and in the South about one in twenty. The church historian William Warren Sweet said of the early days of this country that "there came to be more unchurched people in America, in proportion to the population, than was to be found in any country in Christendom." In 1800 only an estimated 7 per cent of the population were church members. A peak was reached in 1860, when close to one fourth of the people were church affiliated.[2]

The farther west the traveling preachers rode, the less

evidence they found of Christianity. There was a common frontier saying that there was no law west of Kansas City, and west of Fort Scott, no God.[3] Another saying had it that Sunday stopped at the Missouri River. Philip Ashton Rollins, in *The Cowboy*, observed that many cowboys never had an opportunity either to enter a church or to talk to a clergyman. "A fair statement is that, never having been religiously awakened, they were religiously asleep."[4]

"He warn't convicted"

Well into the nineteenth century, traveling preachers continued to be astounded at lack of concern for religion in the backwoods. In 1818, when the Reverend Timothy Flint went to St. Charles, Missouri, to preach, he discovered that "religion was considered contemptable." In New Orleans he observed that "the French people generally came to the place of worship, arrayed in their ball-dresses, and went directly from worship to the ball. A billard-room was near, and parts of my audience sometimes came in for a moment, and after listening to a few sentences, returned to their billards."[5] When William Wood went to a Wisconsin lumber outpost in 1848 to preach, the most suitable place he could find to hold services was the dining room of a tavern. During the first service he was obliged to interrupt a poker game in the adjoining barroom to "borrow" one of the gamblers to come in and pitch a tune for the congregation.[6]

It was the almost total ignorance of religion in some parts of the backwoods that shocked and discouraged the ministers most. One of them told of approaching a man, busy on his small farm, and by way of attempting to lead him to an interest in a religious life, asked him if he did not "want to be a laborer for the Lord?"

"No, thank you," the man replied, "I have a job." And he

[5] Reprinted by permission of the publishers, the Arthur H. Clark Company, from John Ervin Kirkpatrick, *Timothy Flint*.

wiped the perspiration from his face, and set to work again without question or comment.

Preachers were thwarted in their work by many of the backwoods people's lack of a sufficient vocabulary to communicate with understanding on religion.

A traveling preacher told of examining a woman at her home on her beliefs, and asking if she had any religious convictions.

"Naw," she replied bluntly, "nor my ole man neither. He war tried for hog-stealin' once, but he warn't convicted."[7]

A Presbyterian missionary arrived at a lonely cabin in a clearing, and hoping to find some fellow member of his denomination, asked the woman of the cabin: "Are there any Presbyterians in this country?"

The woman, obviously assuming that the man, riding the dim trails through the woods, must be a hunter of animals like her husband, replied: "Wal, I just couldn't say for sure about that. These woods is full of most every kind of varmet, but I ain't paid much attention to 'em. You might take a look around there on the back side of the cabin where my husband keeps his varmet hides, and see if he's got any Presbyterian hides nailed up. If there's any Presbyterians in this country, he's bound to have caught one by now."[8]

Bibles were about as scarce on the frontier as preachers and theological learning. Timothy Flint said of the immigrant families to Missouri that not more than one in fifty had a Bible.[9]

This scarcity of Bibles and the pioneers' lack of concern about them is revealed by a Methodist preacher's account of his offer to conduct prayer at a frontier home before retiring for the night. The host responded by asking: "Do you have a book? We had one, but somehow it got scattered while we were coming out here."

A traveling minister told of trying to sell a Bible to a pioneer housewife, surrounded by a brood of ragged children in a run-down cabin. She was polite in the beginning. When he asked if she didn't think every home should have a Bible, she agreed that it should. Did they have a Bible in this house?

Of course they had a Bible, the housewife answered, resenting the preacher's aggressiveness.

Then the preacher wanted to know where it was.

The woman called the children and they organized a hunt for the missing book. At last one of the children dug up a few torn pages of Scripture. The woman took the pages and held them up triumphantly.

The preacher argued that this was no Bible. The woman contended that it was. Then she added: "But I had no idea we were so nearly out."[10]

When Protestants were heretics in Texas

Religion came particularly slowly to Protestant Americans on the Texas frontier. It was a common saying that side arms and whiskey poured into Texas much faster than Bibles.

The leader of the first official American colonists, Stephen F. Austin, early discovered that frontier religion and politics could make as explosive a mixture as gunpowder—a mixture that could easily lead to the use of gunpowder. The Catholic Church was the established church in Spanish Texas. This made most American colonists, in a sense, both foreigners and heretics. Austin was determined to keep the peace and establish his colony at any cost. Protestant ministers made him jittery. He said that "a few fanatic and imprudent preachers at this time would ruin us." When pressed to be more lenient toward Protestant ministers, he said: "One Methodist preacher would do more mischief in this colony than a dozen horsethieves."[11]

The Reverend Caleb S. Ives wrote of Texas from the Episcopal view: "It is heart-rending to see the field white with harvest throughout this country, and the church, with one exception, without a laborer in the Republic."[12]

William DeWeese wrote in 1831: "There is no such thing as attending church . . . Indeed, I have not heard a sermon since I left Kentucky, except at a camp meeting in Arkansas." When T. A. Morris came to Texas in 1844 he visited in a home of one of Austin's colonists who had not heard a sermon during his ten years in the colony.

Even prayer was so foreign in some sections that older children were puzzled at the ritual. The Reverend "Fightin'" Jack Potter was requested to ask the blessing at a family dinner table when the family sat down to eat. As he bowed his head and humbly asked a blessing, a ten-year-old nephew of the host sat staring in wide-eyed amazement. He was so bewildered at the strange proceeding at the table that he looked the preacher up on the street the next day and asked him: "Are you the preacher that talks to the plate?"[13]

In Tasco, as late as 1886, when four prominent cowboys were killed in a shooting scrape, no funeral was held for them because no minister was available to conduct one. Fred E. Sutton, in his book, *Hands Up!*, gave this eyewitness account:

"There was no ceremony of any kind. There was no one in Tasco qualified to deliver a sermon. I feel sure there was not a Bible or prayer-book in town. At any rate there was no burial service of any kind. Several hundred of us cowboys stood around the yawning graves with our hats off, until they were filled with earth. Then we returned to town, thirsty, and the glasses tinkled, and chips rattled on the gaming tables, and the fiddles tuned up, and life went on as before."[14]

Sutton told of the burial on the bank of the Cimarron of another cowboy who had been shot in a quarrel. His friends stood around the grave with hats in hand, and finally some-

[14] From *Hands Up!* as told by Fred E. Sutton and written down by A. B. Macdonald, copyright 1926, 1927 by the Bobbs-Merrill Company, 1955 by A. B. Macdonald, reprinted by permission of the publishers.

one suggested that Bill had been a "pretty good sort of a scout, and that it was too bad that he had to be buried like a dog, without even a song at his grave." Thereupon a cowboy, "with voice and mien of deepest solemnity," sang the nine verses of *The Cowboy's Dream,* which begins "Last night as I lay on the prairie." He sang it to the tune of "My Bonnie Lies over the Ocean."[15]

In June 1839, two years after Houston became the capital of Texas, a local newspaper lamented: "It is a source of much astonishment and of considerable severe comment upon the religious character of our city, that while we have a theatre, a courthouse, a jail and even a capitol in Houston, we have not a single church."[16]

Actually, the establishment of a church did not bring religious harmony or enlightenment. An organ in the First Baptist Church caused great disturbance. "The consciences of some of the saints were wounded by the presence of so ungodly a thing, and the agitation reached such a pitch that the instrument suddenly disappeared. It was afterwards found in the bottom of Buffalo Bayou which runs through the city."[17]

Even after evangelists put Houston on their "circuits," the city was considered quite worldly. When give-'em-hell Sam Jones, near the turn of the century, appeared in this place he called the city of sin, mud, and magnolias, he reported: "Last week the ladies drank in the drippings of the sanctuary. This week they attended the races."[18]

The establishment of schools did not quickly bring enlightenment. The story is told that a politician, after making a campaign speech near the Mexican border, was asked by a man in the audience: "What do you think of this teaching of the Mexican language to our kids?"

"I'm agin' it," he shouted. "If the English language was good enough for Jesus Christ, it's good enough for me."[19]

Even when organized church efforts got under way, results were not always forthcoming. Jack Potter wrote of his ministerial efforts at Fort Clark: "I went to Fort Clark to preach several years ago, and started in without a member, and at the end of twelve months I quit without a member."[20]

Usually the pioneers welcomed the wandering preachers into their homes and went to hear them preach when the opportunity afforded. However, some extremists never permitted religion to catch up with them if they could prevent it. One settler, found packing his belongings and asked where he was going, replied with poetic emphasis:

> *"Whar the grass grows and the water runs,*
> *And the sound of the gospel never comes."*[21]

Numerous reasons have been given for the creeping pace at which religion came to the frontier.

In the first place, the American Revolution was responsible for the destruction of much church property and loss of religious leaders. A cloud of treason hung over the Episcopal, Methodist, and Quaker denominations because of their support of the British cause. And the cult of Deism and the religion of reason, promoted by such writers as Thomas Paine, shook the faith of many in the old-time religion.

A basic cause for lack of religious development was the pioneer's brute struggle for existence against the harsh elements and savage Indians, with limited, primitive equipment. He was preoccupied with the fundamental necessity of keeping body and soul together on this earth, rather than preparing his soul for the next world.

Furthermore, when he did have time to reflect upon the broader aspects of his surroundings, he regarded any sort of priesthood, or outside tampering with his method of worship, as representing the kind of special privilege against which the Revolution had been fought. Even before the surge for political freedom took men to their rifles, the backwoods settlers were demanding that "the gates of heaven be opened to men in buckskin shirts and coonskin caps." Religious aristocracy died with political aristocracy, or at least the acknowledged system died.

Just as a new system of secular government had to be established by the people, a new order of worship had to be arranged. The common people took political matters into their own inexperienced hands. They did likewise with religion. The religious "systems" of the frontier were not adopted. They were part and parcel of it.

For the devout, the development of the new order came discouragingly slow.

II

THE "BRUSH COLLEGE" GRADUATES

The typical frontier preacher, regardless of denomination, had practiced some vocation, and had been called to the ministry from among the folk he served. He was unlearned, but this was not considered a handicap. Congregations encouraged it and bragged about the humbleness and ignorance of their ministers. They pointed to such early examples of church leaders as Peter and John, "unlearned and ignorant men"[1] who came from the underprivileged classes like themselves, but who confounded the high priests and the rich sinners. The frontier people did not demand that their preachers lead them to knowledge and worldly position but rather to the treasures of the eternal world to come.

The country people were jealous of their new-won freedom, and they resented any attempt of city ways to take over. They were determined to keep religion not only free but simple, and a close personal relationship between each person and the Lord. Theirs was a protest against "coldness" and "formality" within the churches.

Pulpit politics usually demanded that the preacher expound on the sins of those who had more earthly possessions and position. These were the "great big" sinners, an abomination in the sight of the Lord as well as in the sight of those the aristocrats "lorded it over."

No activity so revealed the nature of the frontier people as that of religious participation. They were, in the main, feelers rather than thinkers, believers rather than investigators, individualists rather than organizers, independent in all things, including choosing a mode of worship and a route to glory. Here every man was his own priest, the Scriptures his supreme authority. "Going through channels" to reach authority was not for pioneer individualists.

The frontier folk were not pretentious in the face of each other, and they did not propose to be pretentious in the face of the Lord. The blessings they sought were simple and understandable. Someone has formulated their vision thus: "For the promise of the Word is that some day the children of the Word will find a land of milk and honey where each man may eat of his own vine, sit under his own fig tree and whittle on his own sticks."[2] They were the downtrodden people, the underdogs socially and economically, who could not envision early material emancipation, but who could envision themselves on top spiritually—and for the saints that was what really counted.

Those whose circumstances did not match their aspirations found comfort and consolation in the frontier axiom:

> *Life ain't in holding a good hand*
> *But*
> *In playing a pore hand well.*

The frontier could not delay soul-saving for education and culture to catch up. Peter Cartwright, outstanding circuit rider of his time, wrote of the Whitewater Circuit in what is now southeast Indiana: "Not infrequently a Methodist circuit-rider called at the cabin of a settler before the mud in his stick chimney was dry or before the weight poles were on the roof. It [Methodism] attempted to be present whenever

a grave was opened, or an infant was found in its cradle."
He commented in his later days: "Suppose these illiterate
Methodist preachers had held back, or waited for a better
education, or for these educated times, where would the
Methodist church have been today?"[3]

Just as the frontier folk employed logs and sod and mud
for materials to build their temporal homes, without waiting
for bricks and marble and planed lumber, they utilized the
ministerial material they had among themselves. They did not
choose to put off religion until "better times." And by not
putting it off, "better times" doubtless came quicker.

Some preachers undertook a few courses of reading under
an older preacher, but it was generally considered that if
God called a man to preach, that meant he was ready. A
Baptist group in Mississippi went on record with the rather
prevalent position: if God "wants a learned Moses or Saul of
Tarsus He will have them qualified before He calls them into
his work." This group challenged the world to show any divine authority for sending a man to school after God called
him into the ministry.[4] A Tennessee association as late as
1835 opposed education of the ministry on the grounds that
it implied inadequacy of God and His power to call and
equip ministers. The people, as a whole, regarded preaching
ability as the "gifts of heart" rather than "gifts of mind," and
held that religion was caught, not taught. Preparation of sermons was usually left to inspiration of the Holy Spirit at the
time of delivery. Failure to speak extemporaneously indicated
to some that the speaker had not experienced rebirth.

No Holy Ghost in "book larnin'"

Much of the frontier was hostile to "book larnin'" on the
ground that "there ain't no Holy Ghost in it." In 1836 a
Nashville observer stated: "Our preachers are mostly educated between the handles of a plow, there they have their

study, and hence they know themselves to be much below par." An authority estimated that in Kentucky in 1828 three fourths of the preachers could not distinguish between a noun and a verb. Some could not read at all. Another reporter said that whenever the preachers arose to preach they "usually threw the reins upon the neck of feeling, and let her run full speed."[5]

A preacher interpreting Luke's description of John as "an austere man" explained that John was an oysterman who spent his time fishing. Another said that Christ was crucified between two "Male-factors." A Boone County, Missouri, preacher used for a text, "Peter's wife's mother lay sick of a fever." Three years later in the same church he used the same text. But when he started a man in the congregation spoke out: "Why, Lord God, ain't she dead yet?"[6] One sputtering Kentucky preacher addressing an illiterate congregation allowed that heaven could only be described as a "Kaintuck of a place."[7]

An old Baptist preacher was conducting a revival in the backwoods near the Sabine River. In the midst of his sermon, while exhorting the sinners to flee from the wrath to come a "tall, stove-hatted, high-collared, Prince-Alberted, double-breasted, vandyked-whiskered man carrying a gold-headed cane, came walking down the aisle and seated himself near the front."

The preacher glanced at him, but kept on exhorting. He had several mourners "well worked up at the moment." But unable to resist attention to the distinguished stranger, he finally turned to him and said: "My friend, are you a Christian?"

The distinguished gentleman replied: "Sir, I am a theological professor."

"My Lord," said the preacher, "I wouldn't let a little thing like that keep me from coming to Christ . . . You can't be saved with anything between you and God."[8]

Even the more enlightened congregations took the position that an unlearned preacher was better than no preacher at all. And the ignorant found object lessons from American history to refute the argument for education: Where did George Washington learn the trade of war? The answer was, "On the battleground." And where did the preachers learn to preach? Why, in the pulpit, of course.

Ernest Sutherland Bates, in *American Faith*, sums up the situation thus: "The requirements for the clergy were steadily lowered until they could be met by any one with a native talent for exhortation . . . The last vestige of the European intellectual tradition vanished in the American forest. And in its place developed steadily the great tradition of the common man."[9]

Peter Cartwright, as a member of the Illinois Legislature, introduced the first bill for the establishment of a state university. Yet he had little use for college-trained missionaries who came West with manuscript sermons. He said these educated preachers reminded him of "lettuce growing in the shade of a peach tree or . . . a gosling that had got the straddles wading in the dew."[10]

Bishop Francis Asbury, John Wesley's representative in America, urged those of his denomination upon going into the field to "leave all your vain speculations and metaphysical reasoning behind." It took little encouragement to get cooperation for this admonition.

But in spite of these instructions, some of the young ministers coming from the East were hardly prepared for what they found. One preacher who wrote a book entitled *Five Years In The West or How An Inexperienced Young Man Finds His Vocation*[11] wrote of his eagerness to visit a man of considerable experience in the ministry and learn from him about the work in that field, and get "information from him about how to study, prepare sermons, and conduct myself generally as a young minister . . . I was anxious to receive from my senior any crumbs of instruction which might fall from his lips."

But the young man was sorely disappointed. The elder preacher he found "quite ignorant of the missions . . . Instead of being an exemplar generally, he picked his teeth at the table with his fork."

In spite of his uncouth manners, the young preacher hopefully sought his advice for preparing sermons and received these instructions: "I would recommend that you commit three or four of Wesley's sermons and preach them. Out of these, by hunting texts to suit by properly dividing up, you may make eight or ten; and that is about as many as a man needs. Whenever he preaches he can preach one of these; but frequently an exhortation will answer every purpose."

Sometimes the "sent" preachers found that a little learning can be a discouraging thing. A highly educated but discouraged Presbyterian minister asked a semi-illiterate but notably successful Methodist minister his secret of success in preaching. The Methodist answered: "You write out your sermons, and the devil looks over your shoulder, and if they are good, he tells you you will get into trouble preaching that. Now if you take out all that the devil leads you to, your sermon is so dull nobody will listen to it. Now, my dear Christian brother, when I get up to preach, the devil himself does not know what I am going to say."

Extemporaneous speaking was the order of the times, whether by design to outwit the devil, because of laziness, or to furnish spontaneity.

Many preachers regarded ignorance as no handicap against delving to great depths to manifest mysteries. Parson William G. Brownlow quoted one exhorter, not burdened with academic learning, who addressed his congregation: "My beloved hearers, I shall in the first place speak to you of things you know; second, of what I know and you do not know; third, of things that neither of us know."[12]

They knew what heaven and hell looked like

What the preachers lacked in theology and information they made up in imagination. One observant writer wrote: "They [the ministers] could describe the Kingdom of Heaven more minutely than most men of the present day could describe their wives' bedrooms; they could give a full bill of fare of all the pleasures indulged in there, also a programme necessary to be followed to obtain admittance; but when they came to Pluto's region, they became omniscient—they could dwell for hours on that horrible lake of fire and brimstone in which all sinners, particularly those who lived within five miles of their ministration and failed to attend, were doomed to wiggle through eternity."[13]

Also, many preachers apparently considered quantity a suitable substitute for quality. Possibly the ministers, more than members of their flocks, recognized this shortcoming. Parson Brownlow, a Methodist, made this observation about Cumberland Presbyterian exhorters: "I do not recollect to have ever heard more than one who closed till he was completely out of strength, words or ideas! . . . Of all the deaths that ever any people died, there is none so distressing as being preached to death."[14]

The Reverend Walter Smith South, a Methodist, left this account in his diary of a long-winded contemporary Baptist: "He has zeal and energy, gave a good discourse on the plan of salvation, but never touched the subject of his text."[15]

Subject and organization often got lost in volume and over-generous quantity. Organization and sticking-to-the-subject were not generally considered of major importance in sermon preparation. A church member commented to a friend about a fine sermon he had just heard that lasted "nigh about two hours."

"What was the preacher's subject," the friend asked.

"He nevah did say," was the answer.

When educated ministers threatened to invade a certain section of the frontier further advanced than the average, one old minister in a last fling of defiance and desperation contended that as long as he had wind, he had little need for an education.

The Reverend Timothy Flint, a Harvard graduate, pointed out one cause of this weakness of ignorance in the pulpit when he said: "The lack of taste so much displayed in public came rather from the always common disposition of the incompetent to make themselves prominent and visible."[16]

In this connection it should be realized that, in addition to spiritual inducements, the pulpit held earthly appeals, particularly for the ignorant and underprivileged. The church was, in many instances, the easiest and quickest route to prominence for a man without money, education, or social position. A poor boy with talent who could not go to college and become a professional or businessman could exercise his knack for leadership when the Lord "called him to preach." The church was the one place where he could speak his mind, the place where he could stand equal with every other man before God.

Overnight (following his licensing) he was a welcomed and honored guest in homes, the recipient of the choicest food and the best accommodations available. To many he was the mouthpiece of the Holy Ghost, his words now eagerly hung upon for wisdom to live by.

Responsibility for this condition rested with the people. If a bumpkin, pampered and showered with adulation, became spoiled and lazy the people had only themselves to blame.

The "loudmouth" preachers

A strong voice and voice affectation were generally considered by the old-timers as assets superior any time to book

[16] Reprinted by permission of the publishers, the Arthur H. Clark Company, from John Ervin Kirkpatrick, *Timothy Flint.*

larnin'! They regarded a stentorian voice as more convincing than logic.

It was said of one "loudmouth" preacher that his voice had the volume and carrying power of that of a range bull. Sonorous John Smith of Kentucky could be heard easily a distance of two miles. When high water prevented the Reverend Gardner McConnico from crossing the Big Harpeth River to reach his congregation, he raised his powerful voice even higher than usual and preached so his congregation, gathered on the opposite bank, heard him clearly above the roaring stream. Moses Pierson reputedly possessed a "jarring voice" which "resembled the vibrating of a splinter on a rail fence during an equinoctial gale."[17]

One exhorter kept his congregation in such a blast, it dubbed him "Cyclone" ———. A young boy, puzzled by this appellation, asked his father what a cyclone was. The father replied: "A cyclone is a vacuum surrounded by wind and so is Brother ———."

Exhorters shouted and screamed to emphasize their points of discourse. But the voice affectation regarded as most effective by many divines was known as the "holy whine," by which many speakers delivered their sermons with a twang. They usually adjusted or varied the whine to secure the emotional effect desired. Or, those speaking in the open air, or with great force, utilized it to relieve the strain on their throats. This permitted their voices to rise and fall, and thus provided change.

One Mississippi minister, much imitated for effectiveness, reputedly acquired "the heavenly tone" to such perfection he "could sing and wail out his hymns, prayers and sermons." An admirer complimented Jeremiah B. Jeter as a great preacher who had "most the mournfulest voice" of any man he ever heard.[18]

The preachers themselves were their most severe critics. Through them, mainly, improvement came.

William Vaughn of Kentucky had attended school for

about a year when he was licensed by his church, along with three others, "in a batch," according to his account, "and a more ignorant set would be hard to find. We said 'mout' and 'moutn't,' 'critter' and 'breethren.'" He lamented that some of them never tried to improve.[19]

Flint, wishing desperately to see quality of preaching improved, could do nothing in the beginning. Rather, he had to retrogress, and he himself "became all things to all people, as far as possible." He discarded his notes, reporting that he would not dare under any circumstances to use them, because he found that the "eastern missionaries have very much prejudiced their cause." He observed that the people have a "vast deal of effrontery, and will not pardon modesty in any one. A frothy and turgid kind of ready eloquence is characteristic of every class of speaker." He said he had broken all early habits, and triumphed against his own taste and feelings. To make his mission effective he found it necessary to feign ignorance and discard the habit of modesty.[20]

This man of polish and culture, instead of revolting, studied the needs of the backwoods people, and adapted himself to them, as many others of his kind did. He recognized many ministerial gems among the rough. And where he encountered them, he offered encouragement. A Tennessee preacher was such a gem: "His first appearance is against him, indicating a rough and uncouth man. He uses many low words, and images and illustrations in bad taste. But perhaps, when you are getting tired, almost disgusted, everything is reversed in a moment. He flashes upon you. You catch his eye and follow him; he bursts upon you in a glow of feeling and pathos, leaving you not sufficiently cool to criticize . . . He has the electric eye, the thrilling tones, the unction, the feeling, the universal language of passion and nature, which is equally understood and felt by all people."[21]

[20] Reprinted by permission of the publishers, the Arthur H. Clark Company, from John Ervin Kirkpatrick, *Timothy Flint*.
[21] Reprinted by permission of the publishers, the Arthur H. Clark Company, from John Ervin Kirkpatrick, *Timothy Flint*.

As more understanding critics like Flint came to the frontier and labored patiently for improvement, enlightenment came gradually to the pulpit.

However, many old-timers had to be hit pretty hard before they saw the light, such as the Methodist exhorter attending a meeting called by the bishop to discuss the possibilities of raising funds for the education of young ministers. After listening to favorable arguments, this preacher rose to his feet and said emphatically he was agin' it. "Not only that," he said, "I thank God I have never seen a college."

The bishop asked: "Brother, do you mean to thank God for your ignorance?"

"You may call it that if you wish."

To which the bishop replied: "All I can say, Brother, is that you have a great deal to be thankful for."

It should be pointed out that lack of formal schooling is not the same thing as ignorance, and that the pulpit was not necessarily chosen as a sanctuary for the ignorant. Numerous "uneducated" preachers became notable successes in other vocations. They were keen observers, possessed of native ability, who developed into their own best critics and teachers. The life of George W. Slaughter, who attended school for only three weeks, will serve to illustrate.

Slaughter was born in Mississippi in 1811, and came to Texas while still in his teens as a preacher-freighter transporting Sam Houston's library. He was jailed for attempting to hold Protestant services, got out, and fought under his friend Sam Houston to help free Texas from the tyranny that prevented Protestants from preaching. He delivered Houston's unheeded order to retreat from the Alamo, and later captained a company that helped defeat Chief Bowles and end the Cherokee War.

He practiced medicine and raised cattle. In 1868 he sold 12,000 head of cattle. For seven years he drove herds to Kansas. In 1870 he sold 3000 head for $105,000, and another year a herd for $75,000.

As a Baptist preacher he is credited with baptizing over three thousand persons, ordaining more preachers, and organizing more churches than any other person in the state of Texas.

The laity, too, offered pointed criticism for the clergy to reflect upon.

"Breaking in" was often trying for young preachers who had aspirations for intellectual or theological display. The following anecdote, of various versions, illustrates the typical reaction to obviously educated preachers.

A young college graduate delivered his first sermon to the church that had called him, reading from a carefully prepared manuscript. Eager to know the reaction to his efforts and the initial impression he had made, he asked one of the brethren, after the service, what he thought of the sermon.

"Well," replied this pillar of the church, "as I see it, it had just three faults."

The young divinity school product, stunned at such directness, muttered: "And what were they?"

"In the first place, you read your sermon. In the second place, you read it badly. [No fire and animation, probably.] In the third place, it wasn't worth reading."

Many of the young preachers showed more zeal than judgment on entering the frontier vineyard. One, on his first appearance at a little church in the cow country, found a congregation of only three people ready to hear him. Undismayed, he set forth with all his vigor, and delivered a lengthy sermon in the grand style.

Carrying out his pastoral functions to the last, he stood at the door of the church at the end of the service and shook hands with his miniature flock. Still undiscouraged and eager to know the impression he had made, he asked a grizzled old cowman how he liked the service.

"I guess it was all right," the cowman answered.

At this obvious lack of enthusiasm, the preacher said:

"I'm disappointed that you were not better pleased. I really preached the best I knew how."

"Yes, I suppose you did," the cowman replied. "But when I go out with the feed wagon and only three critters show up, I don't pitch off the whole load."[22]

The choosing of preachers

The choosing, or licensing, of frontier preachers was in some instances haphazard, and even ludicrous. The procedure for "raising up" a preacher was somewhat as follows: When a brother was convinced that God had called him to preach, he made the fact known to the church. The church then agreed to hear him preach a trial sermon. If the sermon proved acceptable, and the congregation approved of his "gifts," it gave him a license to preach in a particular church or small territory. If, after further trial, his "gifts" appeared substantial, and he showed additional evidence of usefulness as a minister, he might be permitted to preach within the bounds of an association. Usually formal ordination was performed only after the tyro preacher received a formal call to a pastorate.

Some would-be ministers preached to groups without formal invitation in the effort to gain recognition. The system was somewhat in the fashion employed by impatient youngsters of Latin countries wishing to become bullfighters. Feeling that they have the stuff it takes, and despairing of formal invitation to prove it, they drop unannounced into the ring from out of the stands with a cape and challenge the charging bull sometimes right out from under the arms of the veteran matador.

This writer recalls seeing one novice tossed high in the air by a charging bull and gored, ending a career before it started. However, there are instances of successful careers begun in this fashion. Courage and ambition have always had popular appeal, particularly on the frontier. Certainly, on the frontier where modesty was generally regarded as a weakness, it was incumbent upon the individual to declare himself. This was the place where rugged individualism was being fashioned. The individual believed in himself first, and this in turn induced others to believe in him.

Examining committees sometimes found it difficult and "heartbreaking" to deny a license to a zealous but obviously unqualified applicant. They employed ingenious devices to let religious enthusiasts down easily. Certainly many examining committees faced delicate and grave responsibilities in informing a consecrated zealot they could not put their stamp of approval on his ministry in the face of his declaration that the Lord had called him.

The story is told of a good-intentioned but idiotic applicant disqualified on the basis of his big feet. He wore size thirteen shoes. The committee rejected him in the light of the Biblical injunction: "How beautiful are the feet of them that preach the gospel of peace and bring glad tidings."

The applicant was puzzled at the apparent inconsistency of the call and his rejection. But he remembered that he had seen the vision that had called him at night while in bed. His feet were hidden under the covers, and thus he now understood that the messenger angel could not have seen his feet at the time. He was disappointed, but now accepted that even in the spirit world these little mix-ups can occur.

Sometimes congregations split over the issue as to whether or not a certain candidate should be licensed. One account states that a church divided to the point of threatening to break up. To convince the opposition of the authenticity of the call, the applicant told in detail how after wrestling for hours with God in prayer, the vision of a man in shining raiment had appeared before him and pointed to three flaming letters in the sky, "G.P.C.," and then said in a still small voice: "Follow these." He had interpreted "G.P.C." to mean "Go Preach Christ."

Following this detail of the revelation, an old deacon rose

and said: "Brethren, I do not deny the reality of the vision. I do not question that the candidate saw the flaming letters and heard the voice. And I do not doubt that the vision came from the Lord. But knowing this young man as I do, and appreciating at least in some degree the infinite wisdom of the Lord, I am convinced that he has misinterpreted the call. 'G.P.C.' in this case, can only mean 'Go Pick Cotton.'"

The interpretation satisfied the opposition, and restored church unity. But it left the candidate hopelessly frustrated. He had never had any such dramatic calls to his other chores, like "Go Chop Wood" or "Go Plow."

Another church found itself in a quandary over the application of an extremely good and devout but moronic applicant. In face of discouragement from the committee, the applicant pleaded that he had distinctly heard a call.

Finally, a deacon seized upon the device of capitalizing on a slight physical handicap of the applicant, a hearing impediment.

"You sometimes have difficulty in hearing, don't you?" the deacon asked.

The applicant admitted that he did.

"Don't you think, then, it is possible that you might have heard someone else's call?"

The applicant admitted that it was possible. But he still wanted to preach.

Whereupon the committee suggested that if the call was definitely for him, it probably would be repeated. Then the committee would take up the matter again.

The account gives no indication of a repeat call.

Visions are more numerous in unenlightened areas. As if ignorance of ministers was not problem enough for the frontier church people, they were frequently faced with the additional bewildering task of interpreting the visions that would, or would not, station their members in the pulpit.

III

BIBLE IN POCKET, GUN IN HAND

Though the frontier preacher was generally poorly educated and ignorant, he was notably practical. He might dream and preach of a paradise beyond the stars, but to walk this hazardous portion of the earth he had to know its immediate needs for his, and his flock's, survival. His people were fighting for existence. Their problem was not how to live beautifully, but how to live at all.

His medium was the idiom of the backwoods rather than the polished rhetoric of the East. He was often forced to depart from orthodoxy and make his own rules as he went along. He did not deal in abstractions; he was a leader by example.

Noah Smithwick spoke of the Reverend Hugh M. Childers as the kind of preacher the frontier needed: "He was an expert with a violin, and even 'tripped the light fantastic.' For an all around useful man he had few equals, always bearing his full share of anything that came along, from a prayer meeting to an Indian fight. A preacher who could only talk found himself out of a job in these parts."

Another pioneer said admiringly of his pastor: "He could

fix a broken wagon wheel, shoot Indians, and talk politics, as well as uplift morals."[1]

William Warren Sweet summed up requirements for pioneer preachers thus: "Western people wanted a preacher who could mount a stump, a block . . . or stand in the bed of a wagon, without manuscript or note, quote, expound and apply the word of God."[2]

Sermons were not composed in "book-encircled rooms," but built up day after day by reflection on horseback, and study in cabins, and composed from personal experience with nature and the pioneers.[3] Being of the people, the preacher knew their everyday needs and views.

Many pioneers, clergy and laity, obviously believed that their spiritual Provider was a practical God who, having placed them amid trying and lean circumstances, would sanction their earthly means for coping with them. Hungry as the folk were for the gospel, their hunger for meat was often greater, or at least more immediate. Thus it was sometimes food before sermons.

A sermon was in progress at a church in a clearing when the dogs that had followed their masters there jumped a bear in the nearby woods. The minister stopped his sermon, listened intently in silence for a moment, and announced that church service was recessed while the men went to the dogs. The women could pray, he said (presumably for meat). The preacher was the first man to hit the ground.

The men mounted their horses and rode off.

After a while the men returned to the church, the preacher took up his sermon where he left off. And in his closing prayer he thanked God for men who knew how to shoot and women who knew how to pray.

Yes, they got the bear.

It was in hazardous and violent endeavors, both actual and potential, that many preachers showed the most courageous and down-to-earth approach.

One preacher on the outer fringe of civilization summed up his views for staying alive and living to do good on the frontier: "I incorporate in my theology this principle—that we are to use all means in our power for safety, and that God interposes only when we are reduced to extremity . . . I believe in building storm retreats, in using lightning-rods, in getting out from under falling trees, and in riding a fleet horse when exposed to the Indians."

He lived by the principle that if pressed to the ultimate challenge he would die with Bible in pocket, gun in hand, and face to the foe—and he lived to write his autobiography.[4]

Jack Potter, after telling how he had dispersed a band of Indians with his Winchester, was chided by the bishop with the scriptural quotation: "Our weapons are not carnal."

Potter quickly replied: "There were no Indians there when that was written."

When the Unitarian leader, Theodore Parker, was called upon to perform the marriage ceremony for a couple of escaped slaves, he realized the hazards involved. But he met the request, and ended the ceremony with about as strange and solemn advice as newlyweds will ever hear from a preacher. Parker recognized that for escaped slaves violence often had to be met with violence. After performing the marriage ceremony he presented the couple, William and Ellen Craft, with what he considered a most utilitarian gift for starting life together—if they wanted to stay together—a Bible and a bowie knife. He placed them in the husband's hands, admonishing him to defend his wife against all crimes. "One's for the body's defense, the other is for the soul's defense."[5]

The problem of predestination

Predestination was one of the most puzzling doctrines for preachers to interpret in the light of frontier needs. But most of them viewed its meaning in the light of expediency.

A neighbor observed a minister known as "Uncle Billy," a

member of a faith that believed in predestination, carrying a gun. He asked Uncle Billy why he was so careful about his gun: "When you meet the Indians and you are predestined to die at that time you will die. So why carry the gun?"

"Yes, I know all about that," Uncle Billy answered. "But it might be the Indian's time."

J. B. Cranfill, in his *Chronicles,* told of a preacher who justified his stand on predestination and gun-carrying in this fashion: "I do not know but what the Lord has predestined that I should kill an Indian today."[6]

One semiliterate minister, pressed for clarification of the troublesome and bewildering matter of predestination, explained it thus: "You see, it's this way. There's an election goin' on all the time. The Lord votes for you, the devil votes against you, and you cast the decidin' vote."[7]

Simplifying theology for unlettered congregations was a constant challenge to the preachers. Negro ministers, in particular, had difficult problems in clarifying Scripture for their people. One exhorter, facing a congregation waiting to hear the word simplified, assured them: "I'm going to make every possible way possible; I'm going to make the roundabout way plain; I'm going to grind the mountains down and make 'em level!"[8]

Many church people never quite understood the supposed workings of the Holy Spirit, in answer to prayer, and for this reason doubtless drew hasty and improper conclusions. But they testified to the miracles, or less, that prayer wrought. A Negro deacon gave this testimonial as to how prayer worked in a practical manner in his behalf. "If I prays for chicken, sometimes I gets it an' sometimes I don't. But if I prays the Lawd to send me aftah a chicken, I always gets one."[9]

Ministers often had to deal with persons who had seen visions, thought they had, or used them for expediency. To find a practical solution, ministers sometimes considered it necessary to prevaricate a bit in the name of the Lord. A lazy neighbor of Uncle Billy's approached him with a religious appeal to try to get some corn from him. He informed the parson that "the Lord told me in a dream last night to come to your crib and get a load of corn."

"Yes, I know," the preacher replied, "but the Lord must have changed his mind. He told me this morning not to let you have it."[10]

The gamblers of Austin built a church

A fundamental necessity for church progress was church houses. Numerous preachers and congregations came by their churches in odd, "practical" ways. Even nonconforming individuals who were not church attenders recognized the practical value of religion for the people and the frontier. The rugged, rambunctious cattle baron, Shanghai Pierce, was not a church attender, but he saw the practical value of his employees' having a church, planned one in detail, and furnished it according to his own taste. Pierce, an individualist supreme, took pride in his pioneering in building a church, and when visitors came to the ranch he pointed to it with evident satisfaction.

One visitor, to make conversation when the church was shown to him, asked: "Colonel Pierce, do you belong to that church?"

"Hell, no," roared Pierce. "The church belongs to me."[11]

To the very last he saw a practical need for the church on his ranch. A few days before he died he wrote his banker in explanation of his losses during a recent storm: "I am badly torn up. I built a nice church for my people all at my own Expense & the Good lord saw fit to give it a H—of a lick & nearly wrecked it."[12]

The Reverend Edward Fontaine went to Austin, Texas, in 1850 with the hope of building a church there. He preached and his congregation listened attentively. But when he talked of building a church they pleaded poverty.

His sermons on faith and tithing brought no concrete results. Concluding that pious "poverty" would never bring forth a church, he decided to approach another element of the city's society.

So one Sunday morning he walked into the Swisher Tavern, braced himself against the bar, and turned to a group of men drinking and playing cards in front of the fireplace and invited them to have a drink with him.

The group accepted the invitation. The Reverend Fontaine was a well-informed man on current events, particularly politics, and a highly entertaining conversationalist. By the time the men finished their drinks most of them had gathered around him. He sat for some thirty minutes more before the fire in conversation. Then he pulled his watch out and said:

"Gentlemen, I am the new Episcopal minister here, and I have an engagement to preach at the capitol this morning. If any of you anticipate attending church services, I shall be pleased to have your company at my church this morning."

The leading gambler of Austin was present. And he was equal to the occasion. Rising to his feet, he said: "Yes, sir, we feel most highly honored to accompany you to church, and we shall be delighted to hear you preach."

According to John E. Elgin, a onetime neighbor of Fontaine, the whole gambling fraternity followed the minister to the capitol, much to the astonishment of the regular congregation.

In a few weeks Fontaine began insisting stronger than ever upon his congregation's building a church. When no action came from them, he called upon his gambling friends and told them he wanted a thousand dollars to build a church.

The next Sunday Fontaine laid a thousand dollars—a gift from the gamblers—on the speaker's desk, told the congregation where it came from, and announced bluntly: "If you so-called Christian people will not cover this amount with two thousand dollars, I will stop preaching to you and go to preaching entirely to the gamblers."

The shamed congregation raised the money without delay, and the Church of the Epiphany, later St. David's, was built. It was nicknamed the "Gamblers' Church."

Fontaine's practical approach to church matters inspired others. One of his elderly slaves named Jake, who acted as his sexton, was a Methodist preacher. This was a convenient arrangement for old Jake. He listened to his master's sermon during the morning service, and then in the evening he delivered the same sermon to his colored congregation. Either these Episcopal sermons were satisfactory for the Methodist congregation or "Parson Jake" knew how to reslant them properly.

One Texas preacher gained the ultimate in personal practicability and independence in operating a church in a manner that may have been unique. He had a habit of giving unrestrained vent to his feelings, and administering large and constant doses of hellfire and brimstone to his congregation rather than considering their wishes. Being more fervent than discreet, he found himself faced with the immediate prospect of being without a church.

But wealth in Texas, from the earliest times, has done odd things for the ministry. The preacher's son had fared sumptuously on Texas resources. He bought a lot, built a church on it, and gave a deed to it to his father with this advice: "As long as you live this is your church. When you die you may will the property to your congregation . . . Now preach all the hell to that bunch you want to."

Practical views of the Lord's work

People, as a rule, talked with frankness about religious affairs. Some, on occasion, took such a practical view of the Lord's work on earth they were not averse to criticizing it as they saw it.

A pastor called on a sick brother whose crop had been washed away and his cows drowned in a flood.

"Whom the Lord loveth he chasteneth," the pastor consoled with scriptural quotation.

The sick man managed to pull himself up on one elbow, both bewildered and irritated, and replied: "Well, I'll be damned if he didn't overdo it this time."[13]

A cowboy returning from an inspection trip across the range during a drought was asked by his boss, a pious man, how the situation looked.

The cowboy said it looked bad, that he didn't see enough grass to build a bird's nest, the water was dried up, and there were dead cattle everywhere. "If it don't rain pretty soon I don't know what we'll do."

The devout and faithful owner replied: "I guess the Lord will send us rain when we need it bad enough."

The discouraged, tired cowboy blurted: "Well, if He don't know we need rain now, He's a darn poor cowman."[14]

A certain hard-working farmer was called on each year by his pastor soliciting increasingly larger contributions for the church. One year when the suggested contribution was beyond that which the farmer felt he could bear, he told the pastor so. The preacher attempted to persuade him by arguing: "Your farm has been good to you. And the Lord has been good to you. Part of this land belongs to the Lord. You are in partnership with Him. So you ought to give Him His share."

The pressed farmer answered: "I acknowledge that the farm is paying off, and the Lord has been good to me, and that He is my partner. But did you ever see this place when the Lord was looking after it Hisself?"[15]

Some church attenders spoke with such lack of reserve and honesty they shocked the congregations.

A drinking sinner, full of moonshine, at the mourners' bench in church, was asked if he could feel Christ in his soul. He shouted with startling directness: "Yes, yes, praise God. I've got Christ in my soul and hell in my stomach."[16]

Complete honesty could be disconcerting. At a revival the evangelist preaching on the sin of hatred asked all present who had overcome this unchristian emotion to stand.

Only one man stood up, a centenarian, the oldest man in the community.

"You don't hate anybody?" the preacher asked.

"No, sir."

"That's a wonderful testimonial," the preacher beamed. "Would you tell why that is?"

"Well, all them skunks who done me dirt, all them scoundrels I hated"—he interrupted himself to cackle triumphantly—"they're all dead."[17]

Doubtless most talk in church was done with pious honestly. In many instances sinners lost all restraint at the point of conversion and confessed their sins freely. But not always. Some cautious converts regarded reserve in church basic prudence, and still thought of the flesh, and the future of it, even while under conviction amid the saints.

A western badman, deeply touched by the sermon of an evangelist, accepted his invitation to go to the mourners' bench.

"Confess your sins," the preacher pleaded.

The badman shook his head.

"The Lord will forgive you," the preacher consoled.

"Yes," the man answered, "but the Lord ain't on the grand jury."[18]

Preachers knew that church talk was not always the truth, and they sometimes told the hypocritical prevaricators so. A Negro preacher was hearing the confession of a young man. In the middle of it he interrupted him: "Wait a minute, wait a minute," he called. "You ain't confessin'. You's braggin'."

Sometimes when members spoke in church without reserve, they had to do some quick thinking to "explain." One brother spoke of a constant troublemaking member at a prayer meeting: "I wish Brother —— was in hell."

The startled pastor interrupted. "I can't understand such an unchristian wish."

"Well," the member explained, "I figure that if Brother —— was in hell, he'd have it busted up in six months."[19]

Many preachers exercised sufficient expediency to turn apparent disaster and awkward situations to their advantage. Under almost any circumstance they were ready with a sermon, and used extraordinary means to get respect for religion. I. B. Kimbrough was traveling over Tennessee collecting money to support young preachers attending college, when he was accosted by two highwaymen who demanded his money. He stood his ground and addressed them deliberately:

"I am a Baptist minister. My work is to go over the state and solicit funds for young preachers . . . I have in my pocket two purses. One represents a collection I took yesterday for this Christian work; the other contains my private funds. I will get down here in the road and I will lay these purses in different piles. You may take my money if you wish to, but I dare you in the name of God to touch the money that has been made sacred by having been given for this cause."

The highwaymen looked at each other and then inquired further of Kimbrough's work.

After hearing him, one of them said: "We will not take either your money or the other."

The preacher decided to push his luck further. Knowing of the general respect held for religion even among outlaws, he asked if they did not think they should help his Christian cause.

The would-be robbers contributed five dollars each.[20]

Many ministers employed a sense of humor with a practical slant. One applying for lodging at a tavern was addressed by the landlord: "Stranger, I perceive that you are a clergyman. Please let me know whether you are a Presbyterian or a Methodist."

"Why do you ask?" responded the preacher.

"Because I wish to please my guests, and I have observed that a Presbyterian minister is very particular about his own food and bed, and a Methodist about the feed and care of his horse."

"Very well said," replied the minister. "I am a Presbyterian, but my horse is a Methodist."[21]

Funerals and headstones

Funerals and burials often created their own peculiar, practical demands. Necessity frequently required that funeral services on the preacher-scarce frontier be held after burial of the deceased—sometimes after months or years had passed.

Ministers recognized that with great distances involved, slowness of travel, lack of embalming facilities, the survivors had to make the best arrangements they could. And the ministers usually went along with whatever had been considered necessary. But one Mississippi minister drew the line and refused to comply when requested by a husband to preach the funeral of two wives at the same service.[22]

Many frontiersmen never had a funeral ceremony. They were buried without so much as a grave marker to perpetuate their memory. And the headstones of the fortunate were not necessarily adorned with statues of angels and inscriptions of gospel inspiration.

Often there were no ministers or meditative poets to compose or suggest fine or noble phrases for gravestones or even books from which to copy models. A fitting or identifying statement was sometimes as much as scant talent and materials would provide.

A group of cowboys lost a comrade in an Indian fight on the Goodnight Trail. They buried him that day, as necessity demanded, beside the trail, without benefit of clergy. The cow camp poet, deficient in Biblical allusion, composed a couplet to be scratched in soft sandstone. It was succinct and to the point, carrying a fitting eulogy and a statement of how the subject met his death. It read:

> *He was young, and brave, and fair,*
> *But the Indians raised his hair.*[23]

Sometimes the inscription writers appeared to get to the religious motif indirectly, or even shyly. But at least they usually tried. Obviously the writer of this inscription to a saddle pal was neither poet nor theologian. It is hardly literary, but its few lines tell a dramatic and vivid story:

> *Here lies the body of Jeems Hambrick*
>   *who was accidentally shot*
> *on the banks of the pacus river*
>   *by a young man*
> *he was accidentally shot with one of the large*
> *colt's revolver with no stopper for the cock*
> *to rest on it was one of the old-fashion kind*
> *brass mounted and of such is the kingdom of*
> *heaven.*[24]

To the conventional-minded and the pious, such inscriptions to the memory of the departed may appear a sacrilege. But it must be remembered that the frontiersmen generally lived, as well as died, recklessly. They lived simply by doing the best they could with the means they possessed. And many died and were buried that way.

There may appear loneliness and religious neglect in such buryings. But there was something bravely and buoyantly significant in the fact that instead of names, the markers commemorated a sustaining sense of humor in the face of adversity.

Some epitaphs carried a funeral-type message for the living, who might pass by and be warned. This one was for a gambler—suggesting the hazards of both clumsiness and avarice:

Played five aces,
Now playing a harp.

Some inscriptions carried pointed advice to understanding survivors—such as this one proposed for gambler Charles Storms, killed by Luke Short—to the effect that bravery was not enough for survival on the frontier. Without skill to back it up, one faced the angels ere many earthly challengers:

He had sand in his craw,
But was slow on the draw,
So they laid him out under the daisies.

This one was placed over the grave of a cattle rustler. A theologian might have phrased the epitaph: "The wages of sin is death." But his lynchers phrased it: "Too many irons in the fire."

An arrangement of convenience provided a touching inscription for beloved Dr. Jones of Big Spring, Texas. When he died he did not possess money enough for the price of a tombstone, and neither did his cowboy friends (he never asked for money; people paid him only when they could or wanted to). So his friends dug up the old hitching rack with "Doc's" sign on it that had stood in front of his office through the years, and placed it over his grave. It read:

DR. JONES—OFFICE UPSTAIRS[25]

Marriage in Texas

Perhaps no ritual, generally regarded as sacred, was subjected to so many arrangements of convenience as the marriage ceremony. This was particularly true in Texas.

Spanish laws and the scarcity of priests in early Texas harassed Cupid's business no end. When officials told couples they would have to wait for the annual or semiannual visit of a priest to get married, they said there were a few things that

one could not delay to suit the government or a slow priest—
and getting married was one of them.

According to the law, couples had to be married by a
Catholic priest, or they were not married in the sight of God.
It was almost impossible for couples to go to the priest. Not
only were distances to a priest considerable; he traveled much
of the time, and thus a couple could never be sure of finding
him at home. Also, he charged a fee of twenty-five dollars in
this money-scarce frontier, where this was more hard cash
than many couples had to start housekeeping on.[26]

Stop the process for rearing families, and development of
the country is stopped! This is the thought some immigrants
said the Spaniards had in mind when they saw how aggressive
the Americans were.

The circumstance developed an odd, makeshift system.
Couples who wished to join their fortunes repaired to the
nearest alcalde's office and had him draw up a bond to avail
themselves of the priest's services whenever he came around.
Both parties signed the bond and went on their way as man
and wife.

Sometimes the couples had sizable families by the time the
priest visited their community. Many frontier sons and daughters had the rare experience of getting dressed up and attending their parents' wedding. Frequently mass weddings were
held, in which many couples assembled, for the convenience
of the priest, to be married in one ceremony. The churchman
got his twenty-five dollars a couple just the same.

Society sanctioned the arrangement. Sooner or later almost
every family was involved, so who was there in a position to
point a finger?

Later Protestant ministers were called upon to marry couples with families. The Reverend Z. N. "Wildcat" Morrell told
of marrying couples in the homes with children serving as witnesses to their parents' marriage. He told of performing one
ceremony in the presence of a congregation, after preaching,

with the bride and groom each holding a child in their arms.[27]

The change from Spanish to United States law did not solve the problem overnight. Out in the wide, open plains, "a hundred miles from nowhere," a cowboy fell in love with a nester's daughter. He talked the girl into agreeing to share a sod house with him. But she insisted upon a proper marriage ceremony, nothing less. But no one knew of a minister within a two-day ride. So the cowhands, determined that love's labor should not be lost, got together, organized, and elected one of their number justice of the peace. In the cow camp the brand book was the only book that could be found. The J.P. was undaunted. Using the brand book as a Bible, he improvised a ceremony to the satisfaction of all concerned, concluding in this fashion: "The cowboy has put his brand on the bride, and they are now hitched to run in double harness."[28]

"Jumping the broomstick" was another way in which couples publicly announced that they were going to start living together as husband and wife. For this ritual the couple stood together, witnesses held a stick—usually a broomstick—a foot or so above the floor or ground, and the couple hopped over together, usually to the accompaniment of an "appropriate song." A writer who witnessed a broomstick wedding reported that the bride in white dress and veil, tucked the veil under her belt for the convenience of the jump.

Even when reputedly bona fide marrying officials were available, the rite was often minus any sacred or inspirational ornaments, sentimental music, or orange blossoms. Quite often it was without even a flower of speech. "Judge" Roy Bean carried on one of the most thriving marriage businesses on the frontier. Occasionally he varied the ceremony to suit the whim of a couple, or his own convenience. But his customers were usually joined in holy wedlock with these words: "I, Roy Bean, Law West of the Pecos, by the authority vested in me by the constitution and laws of the State of Texas, do hereby pronounce you man and wife. And may God have mercy on your souls!"

Not only were couples often impatient, but so were officials. On one occasion when members of two prominent families of Langtry were to be married, the ceremony was delayed because the train bringing the license from the county seat at Del Rio was late. The wedding feast had long been in readiness, and Bean was hungry. So he united the two with a ceremony concluding: "By virtue of the authority vested in me by the constitution and laws of Texas and the marriage license coming in on No. 10, I now pronounce you man and wife."[29]

All justice of the peace ceremonies were not drab. Occasionally some sentimental wit "glamoured" the vows. *The Hammerville* (Texas) *Bugle* quoted this reading of the vows to a local pair:

> *Wilt thou take her for thy pard,*
>   *For better or for worse,*
> *To have, to hold, to fondly guard,*
>   *Till hauled off in a hearse?*
>
> *Wilt thou buy her all the snuff*
>   *She in her little box can pack;*
> *Buy her shoes and extra stuff.*
>   *And feed her on hardtack?*
>
> *Wilt thou comfort and support*
>   *Her good and aged mother,*
> *Aunt Jemima, Uncle John,*
>   *Two sisters and a brother?*[30]

Such frivolous marriage ceremonies naturally led to some lax thinking in the minds of the unorthodox and uninformed. R. C. Buckner, prominent pioneer minister, was an inspiring preacher. In marrying a couple one day, his inspiration spread beyond the bride and groom. Immediately after the ceremony a young man approached him and asked if it would be all

right to borrow the marriage license of the newly wed couple
and bring his girl and get married without further bother.[31]

Another couple came to a minister's home late one Saturday night without a license. The preacher told them he could
not marry them without a license—for them to come back
Monday. The insistent, disappointed young fellow asked him:
"Couldn't you just say a few words to tide us over the week
end?"[32]

Many nuptial knots tied so slipshodly were regarded as very
loose connections by couples who later discovered they had
made a mistake. The arrangement to circumvent the rigid
Spanish system had at least one advantage (for unhappy couples) in that it made divorce a simple proceeding by avoiding
expense and lengthy red tape. If the couple changed their
minds before the priest arrived, they went to the alcalde, de
manded their bond, tore it to pieces, and went their free ways
again.[33]

Roy Bean was the nearest thing to a Reno the Old West
had. He was the poor man's divorce mill. He had no legal
right to grant divorces, as he had no legal right to marry people in the first place. But in the eyes of the population on the
edge of civilization he made a notable success of both.

Once when called to account for his illegal divorce proceedings by a Texas official, he stormed: "I married 'em, didn't
I?"

The official had to admit that he did.

"Then I guess I got a right to unmarry 'em if it didn't take.
The way I figure it. I was just rectifyin' an error and a man's
got a right to do that."[34]

About six months after Bean married two couples they re-
appeared before him, and the spokesman announced: "Judge,
you made a terrible mistake. Pedro loves my wife; and I love
his. We want that maybe you fix it up?"

The judge stroked his chin, and looked at the women. They
nodded in approval. So, after some dickering over fees, the
judge agreed to grant two divorces and perform two marriage

ceremonies for ten dollars—"a bargain if he ever heard of one."[35]

Bean even used his assumed divorce powers to collect marriage fees. One day he accosted an Indian in town accompanied by his still "unpaid-for" wife, and demanded the five dollars the man owed for the wedding ceremony.

"Don't have a cent," the husband replied.

"In that case, I'll have to divorce you," the judge announced.

The Indian said that he did not know what he meant by that.

The judge simplified it: "No money, no woman!"

Whereupon the man said maybe he could borrow the amount from a friend, and started off with his wife.

"Oh, no you don't," yelled Bean. "I'll keep her here until you get the money."

Roy got his money that day. And the couple had the delayed satisfaction of thinking that their marriage was now on the up and up in the sight of God, Roy Bean, and society.[36]

He made property decisions with the same alacrity. A woman complained in his saloon courtroom of the cruelty of her spouse. Bean granted a divorce, giving the woman custody of their burro and giving the man ten minutes to get out of town.[37]

The sacredness of marriage, in many instances, *was* seemingly taken lightly from beginning to end. Fox Campbell, brother of onetime Governor Thomas Campbell of Texas, as attorney for the plaintiff, a lady of color, filed the following petition for divorce:

Mattie Brooks
vs.
Louis Brooks

In the District Court, Polk County, Texas
November term A.D. 1908
To the Honorable L. B. Hightower, Judge,
Of the aforesaid court presiding

. . .

Plaintiff says when a maiden brown,
Old Louis courted her all around;
That he wooed and promised all things fair,
And plaintiff thought him human rare;
And to his words she list intent
And to his wishes gave assent . . .

Those happy days, and oh, how few,
Were destined for this married two;
When a copper colored adventuress fair,
Known by the name of Jenny Blair,
Enticed old Louis from plaintiff's bed
And lived as if Louis she had wed.

The adulterous living here exposed,
Plaintiff says in fact she knows
Began January, 1897,
Railroad time at half past 'leven,
And has not yet been intermitting,
But adultery they are still committing . . .

It is fearful in the winter
To be shivering in the blast
While other ebony women
Are weighing down your mast . . .

Wherefore she prays the Court cite
Louis Brooks hither . . . and decree,
The plaintiff go from defendant free. . . .[38]

And so it went: to provide circumstances to care for affairs of the heart—whether for two to become as one, or two again —the pioneers created some odd, practical arrangements of convenience. The preachers deplored the situation, but they realized that only with patience, and time to work, could conditions be corrected.

IV

EMOTIONS IN STRONG DOSES

It may be supposed that the typical frontier preacher, without formal education, theological knowledge, or training in sermon preparation, was dull and ineffective. He was not. The seminary product, on the contrary, was the intolerable bore and the stuffed shirt of the backwoods. What the "Brush College" graduate, as many of the preachers liked to call themselves, lacked in rhetoric, he made up in expert use of backwoods idiom. His sermons lacked polish, but like their hearty originator, they were pithy, and full of vitality and "electricity, instead of being pale and abstract like the dyspeptic clingers to rocking chairs and book-encircled rooms."[1] And they were delivered with power.

He was not an interpreter of the fine points of theology. Basically, he was a gadfly whose purpose it was to sting the sinful and negligent, a chider rather than an expositor on the fine shadings of Biblical meaning. He hammered constantly on the simple fundamentals—the unredeemed were lost to an eternal burning hell; those who accepted and followed Christ were elected to dwell forever in paradise after physical death. No more vital choice faced mankind, nor could be more stimulating to evangelical imagination. Between the extremes of heaven and hell he dramatized man's fate, over and over, lest he not heed, or become negligent.

He saw humor in his own ignorance, and instead of apologizing for it, he capitalized upon it, and enlivened his congregations with jokes about it. He was a showman in that he studied the materials that would hold the attention of his audiences, and slanted them accordingly. He sometimes resorted to stunts, and lacking in theological knowledge, he employed metaphor and anecdote in the local manner as a substitute. He held the attention of his audience, which is the requisite of any stage. But he was no buffoon purposely clowning in the house of God. He was dead-serious, launched on what he unquestionably regarded as the most vital mission a mortal could pursue.

His aspirations were heavenward, but his ears were tuned to the robust laughter of the frontier where he dwelt. While laboring to "save the souls" of the inhabitants, he also taught them to laugh to ease the inevitable burden of the trials and confusions of this grim earth.

If the pioneer preacher was anything he was colorful, even exciting. The frontier demanded its emotions in strong doses. And excitement was not stimulated by formality. Whether an Indian fight, gunplay on the street, or a gang war, it was usually extemporaneous—it just happened. Here virtually all diversions from the routine of existence, including entertainment and preaching, were homemade and ad lib.

Doubtless, no American stage furnished more authentic local color than the frontier pulpit.

Advertisement for a fightin' parson

Many preachers made fitting and effective use of colorful publicity and advertising. Some "badmen" of the West became preachers. And instead of playing their reputation down, they played it up, in part to present themselves as object lessons showing that a man could never fall so low but that God would hear him if he called in repentance; and in faith his feet could be planted on "higher ground."

Jack Potter was an ex-cowboy and ex-gambler, known from the Oklahoma border to the Gulf as "the fightin' parson." He often employed "advance men" to proclaim his arrival in a town, or to announce the place where he would preach. Once on arriving in a frontier town to preach he discovered that the only available building was a saloon. He made arrangements to use it for the service, and then stationed a "cryer" outside to hawk the service in his somewhat typical fashion:

"Oyez, Oyez, there's goin' to be some hellfired racket here this mornin', gents, by Fightin' Parson Potter, a reformed gambler, gents, but now a shore-nuff gospel shark. It's a-goin' to begin in fifteen minutes, gents; all ye old whiskey soaks an' card sharks better come on over an' learn to mend yer ways or the devil's gonna get ye quicker'n hell can scorch a feather."

Experience led some traveling clergymen to the belief that adverse advertising is better than no advertising. In 1887 two preachers went to Mobeetie to hold services. They tacked up notices about town announcing preaching that night at the schoolhouse. The saloon men tore the announcements down and employed a boy to go about town ringing a cowbell and carrying a banner on which they had written: "Haymakers in town! Come to the schoolhouse tonight." This ballyhoo attracted more attention than the preachers' notices, and the townspeople turned out to see the show—and kept coming. Instead of conducting one service the preachers extended their efforts into a revival, holding two services a day.

These preachers learned that the frontier was for those who asserted themselves.

Numerous preachers not only permitted themselves to be tagged with colorful sobriquets, they exploited them.

The most widely used moniker was "Fighting." Some gained this tag by virtue of a reputation for fighting Indians, others because they battled the devil with such enthusiastic vigor.

A Negro chaplain of a penitentiary who was also a graduate of that institution was widely known as "Sin-Killer" Griffin. Another Negro, who never let confinement stop him from testifying for the Lord, was called "Creepin' Jesus."

Well known was "Crazy" Lorenzo Dow. Bishop Asbury dubbed Nicholas Snethen his "Silver Trumper." One boisterous, uncultured exhorter was known as the "son of Thunder," while an educated contemporary was called the "Weeping Prophet."

And there was "Hellfire" ———, who was not entirely fond of his appellation, and got it for a cause not likely to be guessed. Finding food seasoning on the frontier too weak for his taste, he affected the habit of carrying with him on his travels a bottle of Tabasco sauce. A cowboy seeing him use it on his food one day asked for a sample. The cowboy applied a generous helping to a steak, and eagerly took a large bite to savor the preacher's seasoning.

He almost choked, and water streamed out of his eyes. When he had regained breath enough to speak, he said: "Parson, you preach hell, don't you?"

"Yes, indeed," the preacher answered.

"Well," returned the cowboy, "you're the first preacher I ever saw who carried a sample around in his pocket."

From that day on the title of "Hellfire" stuck to him.

Some cowboy sermons are preserved

A few of the picturesque sermons of the frontier have been preserved. Though some have likely suffered through weakness of memory and recording facilities, a sampling is included here which appears to be true, at least in spirit, and is representative.

Charlie Reed, a cowboy on the Mesquite Ranch on the Pecos River, was killed when his horse fell with him during a roundup. Pony Bill, the "Cowboy Preacher," delivered the funeral sermon two days later beside the grave, under a towering cottonwood:

Day afore yesterday this poor, dead boy here throwed on his saddle an' rode out with you in joyous spirits, singin' the songs o' the ranges. Little did he then dream that he was ridin' into the bog of eternity! While cuttin' a steer out o' the bunch his hoss struck a prairie-dog hole an' fell, crushin' poor Charlie to the groun' an' when you picked 'im up his immortal soul had crossed into the Great Ranges beyond, from which there ain't no back trails. Death loves a shinin' mark, an' it never pitched a rope to a brighter . . . boy.

". . . I say a squarer boy never swung a rope. No one ever asked a favor of Charlie Reed without it bein' cheerfully granted. He war' never known to make a low-down play. He never made a back-set on duty w'en the foreman ordered a ride. True, he war' wild an' reckless, but thar' war' no devilbrand wickedness in his makeup. His heart war' a livin' spring, from which the pure waters o' friendship an' generosity to'ards his companions o' the saddle flowed. He could laugh with you over your joys, an' cuss with you over your sorrows. His soul seemed to be a blazin' fire o' sympathy, to which all who war' chilled by the blasts o' trouble could come an' warm up.

"He war' brave as a lion, but his heart was as tender as a Christian woman's. He would fight like a riled steer fur himself or fur a friend, yet a little child could take 'im 'by the hand an' lead him out of a muss. He warn't a bad man. Did you notice that on the evenin's o' pay day he never j'ined you in your songs an' stories an' fun-makin' at the ranch? He'd git up in a corner and sit thar' writin' page after page, with a look on his face as tender as ever sot on the face of an angel. He seemed to never hear your hilarity, but 'd sit thar' an' write, now an' then wipin' tears from his cheeks on the back o' 'is hand. Nex' mornin' he'd jump a hoss an' ride to the post-office—an' what did he do thar? Jus' an even half o' his month's pay 'd go into a money order, an' the order 'd be put in an envelope, with all the sheets o' writin' he writ the night afore, and then . . . drap it into the box an' walk out with the purtiest look on his face I ever saw.

"Who war' that letter addressed to? To his ol' widder mother back in the States. Would a bad man act that way? I tell you, boys, Charlie warn't a reg'larly branded and ear-marked church Christian, but I b'lieve when the good Lord saw his soul a-comin' up the slope day afore yesterday He throwed down the bars an' let the boy into the Heavenly Corral with a welcomin' smile. I know He did; an' I tell you right now, if I found myself tied to a church or sect as didn't believe as white a boy as 'im 'd get into Heaven 'thout the church brand, I'd take a run on the rope an' break it an' get with a bunch o' Christians that could look over the corral fence 'ithout first puttin' on the orthodox specs.

". . . May the Great Foreman above smoothe and comfort her [his mother] until He calls her up to jine her boy at the Home Ranch amid the Celestial Pastures . . .

"Boys, as you come up to take a last look . . . an' say goodby to your ol' pardner, I hope you'll do some serious thinkin'. None o' you knows who'll be the next. Even now the pale rider o' death may be lookin' you over, and takin' down his rope for a final throw, an' you don't know over whose head the tug'll fall. I'm afeared none o' you'd fare as well as Charlie has if you war' run afore the Heavenly In-spector today. Some o' you think no more o' breakin' the Commandments o' God than you do o' breakin' a bronco, an' if you war' bunched now and started on the Last Drive, you'd leave the trail to Glory away off to the right. Perhaps thar ain't one o' you but thinks he'll call a halt on sin some day, but in most o' your cases I'm afeared Gabriel'll git in his call ahead o' you. Why can't you jar loose from your sins now an' not keep standin' the Lord off from day to day? You'll break the strands o' His rope o' forebearance after awhile, an' hit the bottomless bog o' damnation with both feet an' sink to eternal misery. The fences o' sin ain't high, an' you kin jump 'em. Let me implore you . . . when you stand over Charlie here . . . each one o' you make a promise to him that you'll take the trail to Heaven today, an' foller it in spite o' all allurements the devil sets up on the cross trails along the road."[2]

The unforgettable Clay Allison

Clay Allison was one of the most colorful characters ever to make a reputation in the Wild West with lead slugs and words. He was primarily known for his courage and his dexterity with a side arm. But he had other talents that the frontier never forgot, including those for drama and exhorting. He might re-enact Lady Godiva's famous ride in the street of a frontier town one day and exhort sinners to turn from their wicked ways the next. He had a strange religious bent, and somewhat like the little girl of nursery rhyme fame —when he was good he was very, very good, but when he was bad he was deadly. But whether behind a six-shooter or a lectern Clay Allison was sensational.

Allison frequently expressed his shock at the prevailing indifference to religion on the frontier, a condition that on occasion inspired his evangelical efforts to seek remedy. Once in Pecos, Texas, he had the reprobates of the town rounded up and herded into the Lone Wolf Saloon to hear him preach. Edgar Beecher Bronson in *The Red-Blooded Heroes of the Frontier* gave an account of part of the service. If not recorded verbatim, it is regarded as representative of Allison's evangelical efforts.

Allison began by announcing: "Fellers, this meetin' bein' held on the Pecos, I reckon we'll open her by singin' 'Shall We Gather at the River?' Of course we're already gathered, but the song sort o' fits. No gammon now, fellers; everybody sings that knows her."

The result was discouraging. When three or four had managed to drawl hoarsely through two verses, Mr. Allison stopped the effort for a prayer, which he led at length.

The assembly remained quiet in spite of some restlessness and dissatisfaction. Allison's audiences were traditionally attentive—his gun was always as close as his Bible, and he was regarded as much handier with it. People on the frontier might scoff at the Lord's work and escape retribution on this earth, but it was considered unlikely that Clay Allison possessed such a tolerant or forgiving nature.

He began the sermon:

"Fellers, my ole mammy used to tell me that the only show to shake the devil off your trail was to believe everythin' the Bible says. What yer mammy tells you's bound to be right, dead right, so I think I'll take the sentiment o' this yere round-up on belivin'. O'course, as a square man I'm boun' to admit the Bible tells some pow'ful queer tales, onlike anythin' we-'uns strikes nowdays. Take that tale about a fish swallerin' . . . Jonah: why, a fish 't could swallow a man'od have to be as big in the barrel as the Pecos River is wide an' have an openin' in his face bigger'n Phanton Lake Cave. Nobody on the Pecos ever see such a fish. But I wish you fellers to distinctly understan' it's a *fact*. I believes it. Does you? Every feller that believes a fish swallered Jonah, hold up his right hand!"

Only two or three hands went up.

"Well, I'll be durned," the evangelist continued, "you air tough cases. That's what's the matter with you; you are shy on faith. You fellers has got to be saved, an' to be saved you got to believe, an' believe hard, an' I'm agoin' to make you. Now hear *me*, an' mind you don' forget it's Clay Allison talkin' to you: I tells you that when that thar fish had done swallerin' Jonah, he swum aroun' fer a hull hour lookin' to see if thar was a show to pick up any o' Jonah's family or friends. Now what I tells you I reckon you're all bound to

believe. Every feller that believes that Jonah was jes' only a
sort of a snack for the fish, hold up his right hand. . . ."[3]

All hands went up. And the sermon went on to other subjects.

Many men vowed, when being rounded up and forced to
hear Clay Allison preach, that they would kill him the first
good chance they got. But they usually ended up thinking
that he meant good even if he was bad, or he set them to
thinking of better things than murder. Anyway, no one did,
for his death was about the most unexciting event of his life.
In a drunken stupor he rolled off a loaded freight wagon and
was crushed to death by its wheels.

The colorful Negro sermons

Negroes delivered some of the most colorful sermons. These
preachers often related their personal experiences with striking vividness and dramatic elaboration. The following is an
extract from a sermon delivered at a Cincinnati encampment
in 1839:

"Some eleven years ago, I come to the old camp-ground
[pointing his finger] down yonder in the bottom, in de devil's
barge [meaning a canal boat]. As we come in de range of
de guns of Zion, dey give us a broadside. I was wounded and
fell over board; but dey sent out de lifeboat, and took me
aboard the old ship of Zion, and I, bless God, I on de old ship
yet, and I spect to stay dar till she ride safe into harbor."[4]

Pathos, imagination, and drama were clearly evident in
many Negro sermons. The following sermon (in part) was
preached by "Sin-Killer" Griffin in the Huntsville, Texas, penitentiary, where he served a term for murder. It was tape
recorded by John Lomax. The sermon was delivered a little
later than our frontier period. But "Sin-Killer" was of the
old school; and the verbatim recording of it makes it of rare
value, for it affords convincing evidence of the almost unbe-
lievable native ability of unlearned preachers.

Here an ex-convict Negro preacher in a bare prison hall chanted a description of the Crucifixion. Such poetic beauty might be expected from "book-encircled rooms," but rarely have libraries inspired such unrestrained power and the feel of glory:

Lightnin' played its limber gauze
When they nailed Jesus to the rugged Cross;
The mountain began to tremble
When the holy body began to drop blood down upon it.
Each little silver star leaped out of its little orbit;
The sun went down on Calvary's bloodied brow,
Lightnin' was playin' on the horse's bridle reins
As it leaped to the battlements of glory,
When the morning star was breaking its light
On the grave.

I seen while he was hangin', the mounting begin to tremble
On which Jesus was hangin' on;
The blood was dropping on the mounting,
Holy blood, dropping on the mounting, my dear friends,
Corrupting the mounting;
I seen about that time while the blood was dropping down,
One drop after another,
I seen the sun that Jesus made in creation;
The sun rose, my dear friends,
And it recognized Jesus hanging on the Cross.
Just as soon as the sun recognized its Maker,
Why it closed itself and went down,
Went down in mournin',
"Look at my Maker hanging on the Cross."

It got so dark
Until the men who was puttin' Jesus to death
They said they could feel the darkness in their fingers.
Great God A'mighty, they was close to one another,

*An' it was so dark they could feel one another and hear one
 another and talk,*
But they couldn't see each other.
I heard one of the centurions say;
"Sholy, sholy, this must be the Son of God."[5]

The fast-draw Sunday-school teacher

Conversion of strong, tough men on the frontier did not
make milquetoasts of them. The laity followed much in the
individualistic, picturesque footsteps of the preachers in com-
bining rugged frontier work with worship. Many of the
most notable gun-packing characters of the Old West were
devout Christian workers.

Texas Ranger Captain Bill McDonald will suffice to illustrate. One of the fastest-draw deadeyes on the borderlands,
he possessed a singular reputation for tracking down crim-
inals single-handed. But he also had a singular reputation
for regular and punctual attendance at religious services. He
was superintendent of his Sunday school, and taught a class
of men. Only in emergencies did he permit his law-enforce-
ment duties to prevent him from conducting his Sunday-
school services. And he usually managed to overcome such
emergencies.

One Sunday morning he was called to investigate the stealing of some horses. This could mean missing Sunday school.
So he hurried off in the hope of getting back on time.

McDonald arrived at the church a little behind schedule,
but the assembly was still awaiting his arrival.

He proceeded to open Sunday school, but with only a brief
preliminary remark about his tardiness—an apology for having to ride his horse so hard to get back on time.

When Bill McDonald went after a man it usually meant
news of one kind or another. The men wanted to inquire
about his trip, but the exercises were already late, and the

solemnity of the occasion did not encourage irrelevant questions.

But when the class of men had assembled, one could not resist asking him if he had caught the horse rustlers.

The Sunday-school teacher nodded casually, as he thumbed his Bible in search for the text of the day.

"Anybody get killed?" the class member asked again, his curiosity out of control.

"Four," the teacher answered, and started reading the text.

And then, as an afterthought, he paused, and remarked, as if someone might not know: "I was fired upon."

And the class went on as if nothing extraordinary had occurred and this was all in a Sabbath Day's work, as it truly was for Captain Bill McDonald.[6]

Women were by no means "stand-backers" in frontier religious affairs, though leadership was left mainly to the men. A caricature of the "go to meetin' gals" was furnished by David Crockett in his almanac, in which he represented his sister Comfort, known, from the Allegheny to the Rocky Mountains, as "one of the finest samples of Christianity and womanity." The caricature is, of course, overdrawn in the Davy Crockett fashion, but it was intended to portray something of the color and picturesque vigor that women added to backwoods religion:

"She swallowerd religion hull, an' fed on that an' do-good-a-tiveness all the days of her life, till she war a parfect model of a natural saint; she could preach a few too; her pulpit was the rock, and her sacrament the pure nat'ral element of Adam; her words would make the coldest individual's heart open like a clam in dog days, an' a reprobate's hair stand straight up and bow to her, an' when she sung a psalm you'd thought all the trees in creation war organ pipes, an' a hurry-cane blowin' the bellows."[7]

The frontier never waited for learning and polish and formality to catch up in order to conduct religious affairs. It depended upon its own home-grown ingenuity. On the frontier, religion was of the people, by the people, and for the people.

Religion may have been narrow in its concept, and rough-hewn, but it was never dull.

V

FIGHTIN' THE DEVIL

Vigor and animation was the order of the day in the frontier pulpit. Abraham Lincoln reputedly said that when he went to hear a sermon he wanted to see the preacher "go at it" like he was fighting bees. And apparently most pioneers shared his view. Here, where the labor of the people was often a "death struggle" against the elements and enemies, every man was expected to "put out his all" whether in the pulpit or chasing Indians. A man on fire with religious zeal was not expected to be moderate.

A. E. Rector gave this recipe for pulpit delivery, which he said most of his colleagues followed, or tried to follow: "Begin low, go slow. When most oppressed, be self-possessed. Rise higher, catch fire. Wax warm, close out in a storm."[1]

Macum Phelan quotes a description of a governor's speech which reminded an observer of the delivery of a certain preacher: "He drank water, spit and pawed and with all his awkwardness he was cheered, huzzahed, as if a thunderstorm of eloquence was pouring like a burning river of fire."[2]

It was said of one circuit rider: "If heaven is only to be taken by storm, he is the proper leader for his congregation." Church people considered this type of spread-eagle oratory as "moving" delivery. John Collins, who preached over a wide area of Ohio, was described admiringly as an inimitable tragedian, and "with a soul on fire he poured out the living truth till every heart was moved."[3]

One observer said the successful circuit rider always observed the precept: "The awful importance of the theme should be fully reflected in the *manner* of the speaker. The fire of his soul should be revealed in the flash of his eye. The solemn notes of warning should be re-echoed as with a blast of a trumpet, and every gesture and movement should add impressive power to words that proclaim the fearful destiny of the impenitent soul."[4]

Some listeners were simply overpowered by physical force from the pulpit. At an Indiana camp meeting this stormy type of attack caused an old Revolutionary War veteran to rush from the rear of the congregation toward the altar shouting: "Quarter! Quarter! Quarter!" and falling upon his knees said: "I am an old soldier . . . I have heard the cannons' loud roar, and have seen blood and brains flying in every direction around me; but since God made me, I have never heard such cannonading as this. I yield! I yield!"[5]

Those inclined to exhort in the subdued manner were encouraged to let their thunder roar. The style of William Hickman of Kentucky was admiringly described as "plain and solemn, and the sound of it like thunder in the distance." But when he was encouraged to greater exertion and "became animated, it was like thunder at home, and operated with prodigious force on the consciences of his hearers."[6]

Timothy Flint wrote of the pattern and rhythm of the backwoods preachers: "They did not much affect discussion, but ran at once into the declamatory. Sometimes these flights were elevated, but much oftener not well sustained. For the speaking, the whole was, for the most part, moulded in one form. They commenced the paragraph in a moderate tone, gradually elevating the voice with each period, and closing it with the greatest exertion, and the highest pitch of the voice. They then affected, or it seemed affectation, to let the voice down to the original modulation, in order to run it up to the same pitch again."[7]

Even in small matters—if, indeed, there were any small matters in religion in the eyes of the ministers—they were expected to give their all. Flint attended a meeting of the Presbytery in Cincinnati called for the settlement of disputes, and made this observation: "The ministers took the attitude, and made the long speeches of lawyers . . . They availed themselves of the same vehement action, and pouring out a great deal of rather vapid declamation, proceeded to settle points, that seemed to me of little importance. The whole scene presented, it may be, a sufficient modicum of talent for the bar, but manifested much want of the appropriate temper."[8]

The scheme to bamboozle Satan

Fighting the devil was not always limited to vocal ammunition. Tactical maneuvers were resorted to. James Haven at a camp meeting used a cunning strategem to outwit Satan. He shifted the location of the altar, with the explanation to his audience that "we have fought the devil *there* till he understands that ground as well as we do; we will take him by surprise tonight."

Seemingly, in the minds of the Reverend Havens and his congregation the scheme bamboozled the devil. For the sermon that followed, with its accouterments—prayer meetings in the tents, a "praying circle" out under the stars, hymn singing, and feverent exhortation—"some sixty or seventy were converted."

With the devil now apparently confused by his generalship, the Reverend Haven shifted the service back to the old stand, explaining: "The devil expects us to fight him up yonder

[7]–[8] Reprinted by permission of the publishers, the Arthur H. Clark Company, from John Ervin Kirkpatrick, *Timothy Flint*.

where we did last night but we will take him by surprise again."[9]

Many of the preachers made elaborate and violent display of literally battling the devil in the pulpit, going through the physical motions of picking up chairs and drawing them on the devil as if to threaten him and drive him away from the congregation. Shaking clenched fists in the face of the supposed devil was common. John Granade pictured the devil to his congregation as an armed man gunning for the souls of the righteous. In a furious effort, as if to shoo the devil away by stamping his foot, he came down with such force he broke a floor joist.

A Baptist newspaper in 1840 gave the following guiding principles for success in conducting protracted meetings:

"Let not the dread of novelty deter you from the employment of any measures.

"Bring into the field every instrumentality. Not only the heavy ordinance of the ministry, but also the small arms of tracts, etc. 'Whatsoever the hand findeth to do, do it with thy might.' For who knoweth which shall prosper, either this or that."

These principles were insisted upon "lest while you sleep, the enemy sows tares among the wheat."[10]

They kept them awake

The frontier minister considered it his duty to keep his audience awake, at least physically. Seats in churches then, as is still the general rule, were constructed to promote wakefulness rather than comfort. But if, in spite of the seats, a tired, overworked brother slipped into a restful doze, the preacher regarded it his responsibility to wake him up, and keep him awake.

If making loud noises was not sufficient to ensure wakefulness, the preacher frequently resorted to other stimulants, or amusements, by presenting, or dangling the promise of, a funny anecdote or a pulpit antic before the drowsy listener.

Henry Ward Beecher once phrased the problem in this fashion: "With twenty minutes to wake up the dead, the preacher also had to combat the evils of listlessness and sleeping in church by preaching the gospel according to Joe Miller"—as Beecher was accused of doing.

Beecher once explained: "In our church we have had for some years an able-bodied committee whose duty it is, when anyone is discovered asleep in the congregation, to go at once into the pulpit and wake up the pastor."[11]

Preachers, generally, regarded a vigorous attitude as expedient both in and out of the pulpit.

When Texas seceded from the Union, the German preacher, Peter Moeling, wrote from Galveston: "I shall die a true patriot and a soldier of the Cross, the gun in hand and Christ within my heart."[12]

Another preacher, S. C. Littlepage, wrote in his "Reminiscences" of the Civil War: I "drilled them by day and preached to them at night."[13]

Even in making love the vigorous approach sometimes outed: Texas cowboy J. W. Anderson gave up his saddle and lasso for the pulpit and the Bible, and wrote of both endeavors in a salty book titled *From the Plains to the Pulpit*.

He told of going to church one night, and "while viewing that large congregation . . . I saw two blue eyes which sent a thrill of joy to my heart."

For the cowboy preacher, fresh from busting broncos and bulldogging steers, not even the "climb the highest mountain" stuff was robust enough for his aroused sentiments. With a combination of epical melody of old and "Texas brags" bravado, he wrote:

> *I soon said in my heart, "She is mine*
> *I would bridle a comet if possible for her;*
> *I would muzzle a cyclone for her heart and hand."*[14]

With such assertion we would expect the preacher to win the lady with the "blue eyes." He did. Hands down.

Vigor in the pulpit stimulated and inspired audience participation—sometimes unexpected and sometimes unexplainable. Frontier religion was no spectator affair; it was definitely a participating religion.

It took a hardy voice and often patience to be heard over the fervent shouts of "Hallelujah!" "A-a-men, A-a-men," and "Praise God!" Though the preacher could accept such heartfelt enthusiasm as a token of his effectiveness, and encouragement, he was sometimes hard pressed to carry on his theme with coherent continuity—if actually he was trying to accomplish that.

The audience participated

Sometimes the preacher encouraged audience participation. One preacher started his sermon on the subject of sin, and in the effort to bring his audience closer to the subject, asked his listeners to say what they hated most, expecting such suitable replies as dancing, whiskey drinking, card playing, etc. But he was nonplused to hear a dyspeptic-looking brother in the front row promptly answer: "Indigestion."

Some preachers were quite demonstrative, and even used props to illustrate their lessons. One minister on Temperance Sunday, to offer undisputable proof of the evil effects of liquor, made an elaborate demonstration with a worm.

He first dropped the worm into a glass of clear water where it wiggled about with apparent delight. Then he removed it and dropped it into a glass of whiskey, where it died instantly.

"Now what does this prove?" the preacher asked, beaming with satisfaction.

A red-eyed brother from the rear rose up and answered: "If you drink plenty of whiskey, you'll never have worms."[15]

It was not unusual for preachers to get comments from the audience without asking for them—or knowing how to handle them. A grizzled old trapper came out of a Texas swamp to church and heard for the first time the story of the Crucifixion. The preacher ended the sermon lamenting the tragedy of it, and with a what-do-you-think-of-that look on his face. The old trapper, ignorant of Biblical history, but pridefully steeped in the Texas tradition, rose up and said: "All I can say is that it was just too bad the Texas Rangers warn't there."

It was not considered contrary to decorum in some churches to challenge the preacher from the floor in the middle of a sermon. When a preacher remarked favorably on the subject of shoeing horses, a mule skinner in the audience stood up and took issue by saying: "If God Almighty had thought it right hosses should have iron on thar feet, h'd a put it thar himself. I don't pretend to be a pious man myself; but I ain' a-goin' to run agin' the will of God Almighty, though there's some that calls themselves ministers of Christ that does."

Sometimes the ministers came down from the pulpit to work with attenders and lay workers participating in various ways. In an Alabama revival one elderly sister held out to the last. Nobody working with her in the congregation could quite persuade her. At least, no one could move her to the mourners' bench. Finally the preacher, observing her unusually disturbed condition, came down the aisle where the saints were trying to bring her around.

"What's the matter, sister?" he asked quietly. "Don't you love everybody?"

"Everybody but the damn Yankees!" she exploded through clenched teeth.

"Praise the Lord," the preacher shouted. "She's through!"[16]

Too much action in the audience was sometimes caused by the very nature of the frontier people. They were often tense and restless. It was more than some adults could do to sit still in church. Many chewed tobacco and slyly spat out the window. Some women crocheted or worked buttonholes.

Sam Houston during sermons usually whittled on a soft pine board. According to his biographer, Amelia Williams,[17] it was his habit to fashion some trinket, a pair of entwined hearts, an anchor, or perhaps a cross and crown, which he would present to some child at the close of the service.

Such activities distracted some preachers, but most of them took a practical attitude toward it. A preacher could hardly afford to scold a member for whittling in church when he was regularly called upon to pay more than half the preacher's salary, as was the case with Houston during his later days.

The preachers displayed vigor mainly because, like Abraham Lincoln, that was the way the people wanted it.

A "poet" nailed this doggeral to the door of a church, in which he considered the spiritual fire had gone out. He apparently represented the sentiment of those who looked for action in the pulpit:

A very fine church and a very tall steeple
A herring-catching parson, and a wicked set of people.[18]

If a preacher wanted a live and paying congregation he was expected to enliven it from the pulpit. I. E. Gates, in *Watching the World Go By,*[19] said that people would put up with a sluggish or sick preacher for a while, but they soon wanted a first-class funeral or a change.

The backwoods folk understood action. Thinking came a little harder and slower to them.

VI

"BAD" PREACHERS
AND "BADMEN" WHO PREACHED

Not all preachers met the moral standards expected of them by the frontier congregations, the community, and the established clergy. Some were guilty of hypocrisy, or gambling, or refusing to pay debts, or other forms of worldliness.

On the frontier where people often traveled and changed residences faster than news traveled, checking the reputation of strangers was frequently slow and haphazard. Thus a hypocrite with native ability and physical acquirements for giving a favorable impression might worm his way into society and the pulpit, and so remain in a respected position for a long time before his true character exposed him.

The first Vigilance Committee formed in Houston was composed of ministers who met there in 1837, the year the first church was established. Their stated purpose was to guard the public against fraudulent preachers. No record exists of any dealings with frauds.[1] Perhaps the committee's existence warned the fakes away.

But the committee did not allay all suspicion of newcomers with Bibles. G. C. Rankin, in *The Story of My Life*,[2] tells of meeting a man on the streets of Houston whom he had seen back East and who was running for Congress. When introduced to the politician as the pastor of Shearn Church, the politician said: "Yes, I know him; and what have you done, sir, that you, too, have come to Texas?" The remark was apparently made as a joking revelation of the general feeling of the times.

Another preacher, upon being introduced to a Texan, was addressed in a fashion reflecting the prevailing attitude toward new preachers: "If you are the good man I think you are, the first news I expect to hear from you will be a report that you have stolen a horse, or run away with another man's wife. You may expect all sorts of evil reports."[3] So many impostors and substandard preachers had come to the frontier during the early days they seriously damaged the reputation of the ministry.

The Reverend W. Y. Allen wrote of the needs of the new country: "Men who can preach a little, speculate a little, and make a good deal of fuss about a little labor in hot weather, or wet weather, are not wanted."[4]

Sometimes an undesirable, stubborn preacher got so solidly entrenched with a minority of his congregation he would split a church rather than give up his pastorate. One association regarded a minister as so immoral it proposed disbanding to rid itself completely of any connection with him.

All vocations on the unstable frontier had problems of maintaining standards for their members. It is therefore not surprising that the ministry was no exception. Considering the poor means for quickly checking character and reputation, and the temptations in the wilds to disregard the fine points of ethics, it seems a wonder the percentage of questionable preachers was so low.

The general narrow-minded concept of morals on the frontier, along with decidedly different notions, both among the ministry and the laity, about standards of conduct, served to subject ministers to varied prejudices and estimates. Classification of a man as unworthy of the cloth, or deserving of sainthood, might be a matter of a strict or a liberal point of view of morals by his judges.

Preachers were more critical of their colleagues than were their congregations. If they did not think that a fellow minister was hewing to the "straight and narrow," they attacked him with the same vigor they attacked a sinful congregation.

One preacher visited another unannounced to solicit the opportunity to hold a revival in his church, and found him playing a game of dominoes, and so engrossed in the game he did not immediately confer with his visitor.

The soliciting evangelist was so offended he aired his opinion of the pastor to the effect that he was a hindrance instead of a blessing to his church and community, a man interested in dominoes more than preaching Christ, a Jonah on the ship of Christ.

This same evangelist had no better opinion of another pastor in whose church he held a revival. He broadcast his estimate of the pastor by declaring him unworthy of his pulpit and his high calling. It appears that the evangelist may have been influenced in his opinion as the result of the pastor's referring to his sermons as "rousations" and "all wind," and promising that after the evangelist left, the congregation would have sermons instead of storms.

When an evangelist held a two weeks' revival, and the pastor's appeal for a collection for his ministry there brought in only seventeen dollars and fifty cents, he described the pastor as a "stale chunk of frozen theology."

J. W. Anderson reported that he considered a certain preacher unworthy of a pulpit because one of his sons operated a saloon. Apparently the father had very little control of any kind over his sons, businesswise or otherwise, because Anderson was called on one day to separate two of them engaged in a knife fight while the father stood by helpless. Also, the fact that Anderson was given only fifty cents for train fare after holding a revival in the preacher's church could have colored the evangelist's estimate of the pastor.[5]

Politics often influenced church leaders' judgments of their colleagues. During a heated political campaign over the liquor issue, a church leader said to the prominent Baptist minister, B. H. Carroll: "Hell will be so full of political preachers [like you] that their arms and legs will be sticking out the windows."[6]

Gambling was a problem

The truly immoral or hypocritical preacher should not be confused with the good-intentioned God-fearing preacher who merely possessed some of the weaknesses common to the frontier.

The pioneer cattleman, Charles Goodnight, spoke admiringly of his neighbor, Parson Burns, who was in the cattle business too. He said of him that he would "drink awhile, fight awhile, preach awhile, and swear awhile. But he was a very good man in spite of these faults."[7]

Gambling was generally regarded by the pious as unfitting for a minister. But some ministers were both addicted to the frontier games of chance and adept at them; and in spite of the sporting habit were regarded with respect—in varying degrees. Stanley Vestal, in *Queen of Cowtowns, Dodge City*,[8] related the story of a preacher who regularly visited Dodge City, where virtually everybody, in and out of the church, gambled and regarded it as *the* frontier pastime.

It was the habit of this man to hang his black coat on the back of his chair before he sat down for a game. And then he always opened the game with prayer. He said he regarded chance as God's means of favoring the elect and punishing sinners.

Gambling apparently had hardly damaged his reputation as a preacher until an unfortunate mishap occurred one evening when an unusually large pot was at stake. He was discovered with an ace up his sleeve.

It was not this highly unsporting and dangerous maneuver that hurt his local reputation as much as the explanation he gave for it: he blandly asserted that the Good Lord must have put it there. The local sportsmen could condone a preacher's playing cards, and staking his money on his skill, or luck, for they did not consider men infallible. But they regarded God as being too sportsmanlike for taking a hand in palming aces.

The Reverend James Huckins gave a more severe and representative opinion regarding card playing on the frontier: "A few days since a man bearing credentials genuine and worthy of a good minister, was detected bringing into the country two boxes (containing, as he said, his library) filled with cards and 'Hoyle's Games.' "[9]

A prevailing fault of numerous preachers was a display of less prudence than zeal.

The highwayman preached and Jesse James packed a Bible

A distinction should be made, in fairness to the high calling of the ministry, between the "bad" preacher and the badman who preached. However, this is a most tedious distinction to make. For often one of the most difficult traits to determine about a man is his sincerity, particularly in matters of religion. Some men of devastating faults have appeared to be deeply religious. And perhaps no locale furnished so many examples where the spirit was willing, but the flesh helplessly weak, as on the American frontier.

For example, it would be difficult to say how much of Clay Allison's preaching was clowning and pure orneriness and how much was sincere. And it is just as difficult to judge many others.

For orthodox minds who judge character and religious sincerity by some set of rules, no study can be more confusing than that of the religious life of notable frontier badmen.

Many of them professed religion and were active in church work—as active as their reputations and traveling habits would permit.

The most notorious highwayman of his day, Joseph Thompson Hare, who operated up and down the Mississippi Valley, fought his companions in crime to keep them on the "straight and narrow path." When they did not heed him he read to them from John Wesley's works. He "preached to them to abandon the life of the highwayman."

He had "spiritual" experiences. He saw a vision one night, stopped his flight from a robbery because of it, and was captured as a result of the delay. During the five-year prison term that followed, he spent his time reading his Bible and writing his "confessions."

Within a year after his release, he staged a mail coach robbery and made away with nearly seventeen thousand dollars. Less than a week later he was back in jail reading his Bible, praying, and preaching to the attendants.

He dropped his Bible and said "Amen" to his long prayer just as the noose dropped over his head.

Jesse James, while a young man in Missouri, was baptized, and both he and his brother, Frank, were schooled in the old-fashioned religion. In later life a minister friend met Jesse and questioned him about his wayward life, and asked why he did not mend his ways, reminding him of the example of his minister father. Jesse replied that he would be glad to stop, but he did not intend to stop under a rope.

The minister reminded Jesse that he used to read his Bible. At that the outlaw thrust his hand into his inside coat pocket and produced a New Testament. The minister reported that he looked through the book in astonishment. He later said that never in his life had he seen a Testament so marked up, showing such constant usage.

Jesse's mother testified at her son's inquest that when Jesse left her home, less than two weeks before he was killed, he said to her at parting: "Well, Mother, if I never see you again, we'll meet in heaven."

Cole Younger, a member of the Jesse James gang, was said to have been of a deep religious turn. A niece once said to a biographer: "Uncle Cole liked to read . . . He liked theological works . . . You know he was always deeply religious, probably would have been a minister if the war hadn't come along and changed everything for him."

John Wesley Hardin was also the son of a preacher, and it is said he followed the paternal example so far as to study theology. He was reputedly a good Sunday-school teacher at the penitentiary.

Al Jennings was reportedly a Bible scholar and an excellent prison Sunday-school teacher.

Big-time gangster used the pulpit

The supreme example of the badman who preached was John A. Murrell. It is ironical that this most diabolical criminal of his day, the first big-time American gangster, was one of the most impressive pulpit orators of his century.

Murrell was a product of his times. He saw, perhaps better than anyone else, how the frontier folk could be hoodwinked and deceived in the name of religion, how blind respect could be gained by a long face, a long coat, and the ability to shout Scripture. He was the most ingenious and determined of the religious charlatans of the American frontier.

John A. Murrell was the son of a thieving, aristocrat-hating mother and a lazy, henpecked preacher-father. As a child growing up on the Natchez Trace in Tennessee he was impressed by the blind confidence a minister of the gospel could inspire, even a sorry minister like his father.

As a young man Murrell was apprehended for horse stealing, lashed at the public whipping post, branded, and sentenced to prison. At this cruel punishment he declared eternal vengeance upon society. While in prison he studied theology and law, and prepared himself well for his avowed vengeance.

Out of prison he assumed the garb and manner of an evangelist, and he studiously perfected the tricks of his trade. To horse rustling he added slave stealing and passing counterfeit money.

He never carried off property himself. He kept with him a corps of assistants to attend to details of the work. His assistants stood by incognito while the evangelist indicated his choice of horseflesh as he mingled with the good people in somewhat the following manner:

"Glad to see you tonight, Brother Jones," he would say over a firm handclasp. Or, "Brother Brown, I see you are a good judge of horses. I'd sure like to own an animal like that."

In this manner he would greet the members of his congregation, and thus select perhaps a dozen of their best horses. And while he exhorted the sinners to repentance, and pointed out to them the way of the light, his anonymous assistants would be saving the best horses from the hitching rack for the evangelist. The tall, sanctimonious man in the long coat who held on so tenderly to his black-backed book would have been the last man suspected.

Also, church people were not inclined to examine with any care the paper money an evangelist passed out.

On one of his tours, according to his report, he visited some of the larger towns of the country, including Lexington, Richmond, Charleston, Savannah, and Augusta. At the end of the revival campaign he summed up his accomplishments as follows:

"In all the route I robbed only eleven men, but I preached some mighty fine sermons, and scattered a good deal of counterfeit United States paper money among the brethren."

One of his choice tricks was to have a favorite body servant named Tip fall in love with one of the Negro girls in the community where he preached. Feigning tender-heartedness, Murrell would permit himself to be persuaded in the interest of true love to part with his favorite slave. When the preaching was over, the honeymoon was over, and Tip, following orders, abandoned his bride to repeat the performance at the next stand. When the repeating bridegroom became too well known, Brother Murrell, for basic security reasons, pledged him to eternal secrecy with a charge of buckshot and sank his body in the Mississippi River, as was his custom for handling robbery victims.

Murrell made one departure from general ministerial custom. He took no sackcloth-and-ashes attitude concerning attire for the ministry. He was one of the best-dressed men of his day, whether in the pulpit or relaxing in the red-light districts of the river towns.

His most diabolical scheme was to plot a slave rebellion, which he subtly organized on his preaching tours. He led the slaves to believe that he could lead them to their deserved freedom by murdering their masters. He headed a highly organized gang by this time, probably the largest in American history, members of which would captain troops of black slaves—not for freedom, but to pillage the South, the land of the aristocrats his mother had taught him to hate.

As might be expected, loyal slaves got the information and told their masters. By clever detective work Murrell was apprehended. And clever lawyer that he was, along with three other outstanding lawyers, he got off with a ten-year sentence in the penitentiary at Nashville on a charge of slave stealing.

After his confinement in 1834, reports came out from the penitentiary that he spent his time free from prison labor poring over his Bible. Some have surmised that Murrell, in converting multitudes, converted himself in the process. This does not seem likely, though it is reported that he spent his last days, after serving his sentence, reading his Bible and living a quiet and peaceful life.

No one so successfully used the pulpit to promote crime as John A. Murrell.[10]

Ignorance and blind faith on the frontier being what it was, Murrell, more than anyone else, demonstrated that perhaps the safest place for a clever charlatan or crook to hide was in the pulpit.

VII

CAMP MEETINGS AND GREAT REVIVALS

At the turn of the nineteenth century the backwoods literally burst into spiritual flame. The instrument of this great awakening was the camp meeting. An observer in 1801 described the revival as "a fire that has long been confined—bursting all its barriers and spreading with a rapidity that is indescribable."[1]

Following the Revolution, John Wesley had sent his circuit riders into the wilderness plodding wearily on horseback from cabin to cabin, and then from church to church. They, along with the rough, self-taught Baptists, and the slightly more formal Presbyterians, for years carried the torch of religion, bringing light to an individual here, and perhaps a family there, but the light was a mere flicker, often going out with their passing. As the eighteenth century wore on, the pious in their discouragement regarded the frontier as abandoned to "worldliness, immorality, and infidelity."

Just why the great revival started at this particular time is too complex to attempt to answer here. But once started the preachers fed it emotional fuel until it engulfed the country in an emotional upheaval never before known on this continent.

A few obvious factors contributed to this explosion of passion: the wilderness was, in a sense, an emotional vacuum. The pioneers had long been preoccupied with the physical struggle for existence—building a cabin or sod house, clearing land for crops, fighting off the savages. Ceaseless hard labor in their isolated clearings left little time for social affairs, amusements, or spiritual gratification. Life was monotonous.

The pioneer was geared to emotional action rather than meditative calculations. He possessed neither training nor time for the latter. He was processed for quick response to stimuli in his wilderness of unpredictable and violent suddennesses—Indian raids with loss of life and fortune, flash floods, windstorms, grass fires that swept ranges away, parching sun that took both water and food from man and stock in a few days.

Settlement of disputes was made in the quick flash of gunpowder or a blade.

For a society emotionally, socially, and spiritually starved, the camp meeting was the most compelling attraction that ever came its way. It brought the people together from their scattered woodland voids with the impact of atomic fusion.

Here was presented with melodramatic simplicity the supreme drama of man—his acceptance or rejection of salvation. For those who heeded the Scriptures and gave up the desires of the flesh, a personalized God offered eternal glory and cessation from struggle in a paradise of pearly gates and golden streets. The fate of those who rejected the Word was everlasting torment by a personalized devil in a flaming lake of fire and brimstone.

The sustained impact upon simple minds facing this terrible decision, along with a feeling of inadequacy to merit salvation, was often more than either nerves or spirit could endure with normalcy.

Even small meetings in homes could be terrifying affairs

for those who had the inclination or capacity to meditate at length on "the great decision." An observer told of attending such a gathering in Virginia: The leader "dwelt on the awful subject of the judgement to come . . . She (a member of the assembly) trembled as if the judge was at the door . . . I solemnly surveyed the house . . . and it is a fact, that the floor was as wet with tears of the people, as if water had been sprinkled all over it, or with a shower of rain."[2]

Camp meetings were conducted on a larger and grander scale than any other enterprise on the frontier. As one observer said: "Races, fairs, and monkey shows were fairly small concerns."[3] A clearing in the forest, or a pasture, served as a gathering place. The central meeting site was established, and tent "cities" went up around it. All the facilities for living—cooking, sleeping, sanitation—had to be arranged at the site.

The entire population poured into these clearings as if they were true social vacuums—the pious and the scoffers, curiosity seekers, whiskey peddlers—they all came because the camp meeting was the most exciting event going on. People came flocking in from long distances, from everywhere—on foot, horseback, in fine carriages, ox carts, covered wagons: poor man, rich man, white man, and black man. The camp meeting was the social as well as the spiritual melting pot of the frontier. Here all stood before the common altar of God —but with different poses, at least in the beginning.

The Reverend James B. Finley, who witnessed many of the meetings, wrote of one in Kentucky where some twenty-five thousand people gathered. He counted seven ministers, all preaching at one time from wagons, stumps, or fallen trees. He commented that the noise was "like Niagara."

This description of a meeting in Hancock, Georgia, is perhaps more representative of size: ". . . We counted thirty-seven Methodist preachers at the meeting; and with the assistance of a friend I took an account of the Tents, and there were some hundred and seventy-six of them, and many were very large. From the number of people who attended preaching at the rising of the sun, I concluded that there were about 3,000 persons, white and black to-gether, that lodged on the grounds at night . . .

"We fixed the plan to preach four times a day—at sunrise, 10 o'clock, 3 o'clock, and at night, and in general we had an exhortation after the sermon . . .

"The ground was laid out in a tolerable convenient place, containing four or five acres, and the Tents were pitched close to each other; yet the ground only admitted of about 120 Tents in the lines; the other Tents were pitched behind them in an irregular manner. We had plenty of springs convenient to supply men and beasts with water."[4]

The high pitch of emotionalism

Regardless of size or physical layout of the grounds, once the meeting got under way, chain reactions of emotionalism swept the people up in uncontrolled storms of passion. The high-pitched emotionalism of the meetings took on some odd manifestations. In the mass hysteria of the shouting, groaning, agitating sessions, with the ministers declaring the narrow ledge that separated the lost from eternal damnation, with a multitude of the "saved" pleading in a great continuing babble with the sinners to turn from the eternal fire that was just a heartbeat away, people often lost control of themselves under the strain.

Services often lasted for hours, and have been described as a "frothing frenzy," with men and women going into emotional fits. In some meetings the people clapped their hands in a loud, primitive hypnotic rhythm. Screams and shouts were common.

An eyewitness at a Virginia camp meeting saw "multitudes,

[4] Reprinted by permission of the publishers, the Arthur H. Clark Company, from Ulrich B. Phillips, ed., *Plantation and Frontier Documents*.

some roaring on the ground, some wringing their hands, some in ecstasies, some praying, some weeping; and others so outragiously cursing and swearing that it was thought they were really possessed of the devil."[5]

James B. Finley wrote of a Cane Ridge, Kentucky, service: "At one time I saw at least 500 swept down in a moment, as if a battery of a thousand guns had opened upon them, and then immediately followed shrieks and shouts that rent the very heavens. My hair rose up on my head."[6] Another preacher said that the sobs, groans, and cries of the penitents reminded him of a battlefield after a heavy battle.

"Everything was done to produce a boiling heat, the 'singing ecstasies' served to add fuel to the fire; a brother would be called on to pray who roared like a maniac. The male part of the audience groaned, the female portion shrieked; worshippers would begin falling . . . The wicked feared and often succumbed to the spell."[7]

Once a meeting got under way the emotional momentum might carry it through the night into the next day. "The minister would scarcely have an opportunity to sleep; sometimes the floor would be covered with persons struck down under conviction for sin. It frequently happened that when they had retired to rest at a late hour, they would be under the necessity of arising again, thro' the earnest cries of the penitent."[8]

When the meeting reached its height, "every tent became a 'bethel of struggling Jacobs and prevailing Israels,' every tree 'an altar,' and every grove a 'secret closet.' "[9]

The "jerks" and the falling exercises

One of the most common bodily agitations was an exercise known as the "jerks." Moore and Foster, in *Tennessee, the Volunteer State, 1769–1923,* gave this firsthand description: "Sometimes the subject of the jerks would be affected in some one member of the body, sometimes in the whole system.

When the head alone was affected, it would be jerked backwards and foward in quick successions, the head nearly touching the ground behind and before. Though so awful to behold, I do not remember that any one of the thousands I have seen thus affected ever sustained any injury in body."[10]

Parson William G. Brownlow spoke of the jerks as an instrument of conversion: "We had a shaking, and some souls felt convicting and converting grace." But he admitted to their severity: ". . . bonnets, hats and combs of ladies fly off so violently did their heads jerk back and fourth . . . People jerked so violently they . . . had kicked up the earth as a horse stamping flies."[11]

Peter Cartwright, though a camp meeting exhorter of the first water, attempted to "remedy" the jerks rather than encourage them. He apparently regarded this type of seizure as a hazardous by-product of the revivals. To him, when the dressed-up aristocrats took the jerks they appeared a bit ludicrous. He wrote of them in his autobiography: "To see those proud gentlemen and young ladies, dressed in their silks, jewelry and prunella, from top to toe, take the jerks would often excite my risibilities. The first jerk or so, you would see their fine bonnets, caps and combs fly; and so sudden would be the jerking of the head that their long hair would crack almost as loud as a waggoner's whip."

He described one seizure that resulted in the death of the subject: "At length he fetched a very violent jerk, snapping his neck, fell, and soon expired, with his mouth full of cursing and hellenness. I always looked upon the jerks as a judgment sent from God, first to bring sinners to repentance; and secondly to show professors that God could work with or without means. It was my practice to recommend fervent prayer as a remedy, and it almost universally proved an effective antidote."[12]

The falling exercises were another common manifestation: "The subject of this exercise would generally, with a piercing scream, fall like a log on the floor or earth, and appear as dead."[13]

Subjects fell in various manners. Flint wrote of the exercises: "The vertical column (of a young lady) was completely pliant, her body, her neck, and her extended arms, bent in every direction successively. It would be impossible to describe the diversity of cases . . . The scene to me was equally novel and curious."

Multitudes fell in mass. Subjects were seized with varying intensity and for various lengths of time. Scoffers as well as penitents were "mowed down." Finley told in his autobiography of an attack of a scoffer who rode his horse into a circle of praying people:

"Suddenly, as if smitten by lightning, he fell from his horse . . . He exhibited no signs whatever of life, his limbs were rigid, his wrists pulseless, and his breath gone. Several of his comrades came to see him, but they did not gaze at him long till the power of God came upon them, and they fell like men slain in battle . . . I watched him closely for thirty hours, to all human appearances dead. At last he exhibited signs of life, but they were fearful spasms, which seemed as if he were in a convulsive fit, attended by frightful groans, as if he were passing through the intensest agony . . . finally convulsions ceased, and springing to his feet, his groans were converted into loud and joyous shouts of praise . . . a happy smile lighted up his countenance."[14]

Trances usually lasted longer than other manifestations, and to some observers were the most weird. Many subjects lay as if dead, even for days, and afterward related many extraordinary happenings observed or experienced "out of this world."

A contemporary said of the milder trances that sometimes when the subjects were unable to stand or sit "they have the use of their hands, and can converse with perfect composure. In other cases they are unable to speak, the pulse becomes weak, and they draw a difficult breath about once a minute;

in some instances their extremities become cold, and pulsation, breathing, and all signs of life forsake them for nearly an hour. Persons who have been in this situation have uniformly avowed that they felt no bodily pain; and that they had the entire use of their reason and reflection, and that when they recovered, they could relate everything that had been said or done near them . . . Some had seen visions, heard unspeakable words, smelled fragrant odors and had a delightful singing in their breast."[15]

Peter Cartwright considered trances troublesome, especially the more gripping ones. In some instances, it appears, the revelations of the trance "victims" overshadowed disclosures from the pulpit. Those who had experienced trances became persons apart and held greater sway for a time than the ministers. It is understandable that this caused some scoffing from the clergy. To Cartwright this trance business was a nuisance.

He wrote: "They prefer to fall into trances and see visions, and lay apparently motionless for days, sometimes for weeks at a time without food or drink, and when they come to, they profess to have seen heaven and hell, to have seen God, Angels, the devil, and the damned, and often predicted the time of the end of the world." Cartwright considered these predictions of the date of the end of the world as the most troublesome revelations of all.[16]

He spoke of one trance from which the subject never recovered, a woman "who lingered for thirteen days and nights, and then died without ever returning to her right mind."

Cartwright reported that a few persecutors and opposers of the Methodists tried to make a great fuss about the affair, but they were afraid to go forward with it "for fear the Lord would send the same affectation on them."[17]

The running exercises may have had various stimuli. In any event, the subject appeared to have lost control of himself, at least partially, and ran because of extreme nervousness, pent-up energy, or fright. Many under extreme agitations, through fear, attempted to run away and thus escape them. Sometimes they ran considerable distances. But more often they did not run far before they fell, and became so agitated they could not proceed farther.

Religious agitations took frightful forms. Some people were possessed with barking attacks. Those possessed often ran away from the meeting places into the woods and barked up a tree. This was known as "treeing the devil." The barking exercises, according to some contemporary reporters, was a result of the jerks. A person affected with the jerks, especially in the head, would often make a grunt or bark, from the suddenness of the jerk.

The dancing exercise was both wonderful and startling to some observers. The afflicted one, apparently unable to contain himself, went into various excited rhythms, sometimes to the point of exhaustion.

The singing exercise was almost unanimously regarded as the most wonderful of all. An authority on the subject said: "The singing exercise is more unaccountable than anything I ever saw."[18] The subject, in an extremely happy frame of mind, would sing melodiously, not from the mouth or nose, but entirely from the breast. It was generally described as heavenly.

Religious manifestations were extensive. In some locales it was common to see people playing on imaginary harps.

The laughing exercise, usually called the "holy laugh," was confined to the religious, more often the preachers. Flint reported, not too sympathetically that nothing was more common at the meetings than to see forward people indulging in what seemed an idiotic and spasmodic laugh!

Some viewed it skeptically

Scoffers, as well as many of the religious, claimed that the camp meeting exerted a bad influence both upon the individual and society in general. While the "muscular Christianity" of "unbridled emotionalism" was in progress among the saints and penitents about the main stand, other elements of society were taking in the revival in other ways that were far from reverent.

Parson Brownlow said that "announcement of a camp meeting brought glee to the hearts of the bullies, drunkards, pickpockets, horsethieves, and whiskey traffickers throughout the surrounding country."[19]

Keating said of Tennessee meetings: "The town and country sent its thousands to swell the crowd, which found ample provisions for its comfort, including a dozen or more booths in different directions, a quarter of a mile or less from the main shed, composed of bushes cut and piled up, behind which was concealed a barrel of whiskey. The proprietors were supplied with an ample number of junk bottles and runners to attend the customers at the shed, where the bottles would be passed around, sometimes within a few yards of the speaker's stand, until their contents were exhausted, when they would be dispatched back with the necessary fee for refilling; and its effects may be readily imagined."[20]

Jokes were legion about the confusion of corn spirits and the Holy Spirit. A typical burlesque testimonial of the period ends: "I'm sanctified through and through—and plumb full of bug juice."

The gatherings served to some extent as an athletic meet in those days when sports were not organized. One contemporary wrote: "While they [the men] were about these wagons, they learned to run, jump, wrestle, play, yell, swear, talk vulgar." Card playing and horse racing were common in the vicinity.

Camp meetings served as trading marts—though not designed for such. These gatherings drew promoters and speculators eager for a quick dollar. Horses and liquor probably made up the heaviest traffic. But many types of merchants are mentioned in contemporary annals—some selling gingerbread, watermelons, corn, lemonade, books, pots and pans.

Barbers, photographers, bootblacks, and doctors set up shop. Criticism was directed at one man who announced on the camp grounds his availability for "pulling teeth." A preacher was criticized because he announced that a friend had shoe-blacking on the grounds for sale.

Probably the most prosperous business was done by a sales-man who promised for his product "speedy and gratuitious relief from the headache."

The sexual excitement

Sexual offenses associated with the camp meetings brought the most severe criticism—at least they were the source of the most adverse talk.

The people joyfully sang "The Old Time Religion . . . makes me love everybody" without thinking perhaps that love for everybody might not be limited entirely to spiritual love. John Humphrey Noyes, the nineteenth-century philoso-pher who tried to reason out the close connection between emotional preaching and the breaking of the prevailing code, stated that the conclusion was apparent that "religious love is the very near neighbor of sexual love and they always get mixed up in the intimacies and social excitement of re-vivals. The next thing a man wants, after he has found salva-tion for his soul, is to find his Eve and his Paradise."

Keating said of the social aspects of camp meetings that they drew all sorts, "particularly the women, who, of course, drew the men . . . The very homeliest woman in the country could get as many beaux as she wanted, while the beauties wielded a sway that was truly distressing . . . There may be some who think that a camp meeting is no place for love-making; if so they are much mistaken. When the mind be-comes bewildered and confused, the moral restraints give way, and the passions are quickened and less controllable. For a mile around a camp ground the woods seem to be alive with people; every tree or bush had its group or couple, while hundreds of others in pairs were seen prowling around in search of some cozy spot."[21]

What many girls remembered most vividly of the revivals and wrote about to their friends was that "we had beaux in abundance." One wrote that all the young women enjoyed themselves "more than they ever had before."

Some observers did not have to look farther than the religious services at the stands to get shocked. Frances Trollope, the English traveler and writer, was appalled by the indecorum of the proceedings and by the "open display of sexuality . . . More than once (at Cincinnati) I saw a young neck encircled by a reverend arm."

In writing of girls losing control of themselves she observed one ". . . her face pale as death; her eyes wide open, and perfectly devoid of meaning; her chin and bosom wet with slaver; she had every appearance of idiotism." She saw a preacher approach the girl. "He took her delicate hand, 'Jesus is with her! Bless the Lord!' he said and passed on."[22]

One visitor reported that courting had started, or was continuing, at breakfast. She gave this commentary on the morning after: "I marked many a fair but pale face, that I recognized as a demoniac of the night, simpering beside a swain, to whom she administered coffee and eggs."

Observers indicated that women were more excitable and prone to lose control of themselves at the meetings than men. Women probably were no more indiscreet or lax in their conduct than men, but their actions, understandably, created more notice.

One visitor, noting that women particularly were affected at the meetings, stated that in the transport of their feelings they hugged and kissed everybody in their vicinity. (The excitement seemed to afford the same license or lack of self-control as winning a prize on modern television.) Another visitor stated that women in their frantic agitations sometimes "unconsciously tore open their bosoms and assumed indelicate attitudes."[23]

Frances Trollope described a multitude at prayer, mainly women, who fell on their knees; "but this posture was soon changed for others that permitted greater scope for convulsive movement of their limbs; and they were soon lying on the ground in an indescribable confusion of heads and legs." She said they threw their limbs about with incessant and violent motion.

There are reports of the camp meeting excitement bringing specific, sad complications, even among the ministry. A traveling author commented on the excitable women, who assumed indelicate female attitudes in the house of the Lord, exciting at least one minister to sin.

The Reverend John Lyle, a Presbyterian, was a critic of the camp meeting emotionalism. He was distressed that its influence had invaded his congregation. He observed that some of the women who were the most persistent victims of the falling exercises were the ones prone to forget the edict of virtue. Thus, he lamented, "Becca Bell, who often fell, is now big with child to a wicked trifling school master of the name of Brown who says he'll be damned to hell if he ever marries her." He lamented on the condition of another of his female parishoners, Polly Moffitt, who "got careless" and was "with child to Petty and died miserably in child bed."[24]

No amount of piousness and good efforts from the pulpit could overcome the ugly stories about "camp meeting babies." A persistent one concerned the community doctor who advised the evangelists to shut up shop since they were making souls faster than they were saving them.

Ernest Sutherland Bates in *American Faith* states that the sexual basis of the camp meeting orgies is too obvious to be overlooked. He said that in spite of all the exuberance of frontier life there was no frank recognition of the natural impulses, that the body was still denounced as the source of sin, that sex was still insulted, and that men still tried to convince themselves that they married and had children solely through a sense of duty. Thus, when the repressed natural impulses could be dammed up no longer, they found expression, where "with howlings and rollings and sexual convulsions, souls were converted to God. The camp meeting afforded in more violent form the same emotional katharsis achieved in more settled societies through music, the drama, and the dance."[25]

Criticism of the camp meetings came from a number of specific sources.

Foreigners, particularly the British, interpreted the meetings as evidence of the license resulting from the American system of democracy. To them, the meetings showed disorder, lack of taste, and emotional instability. One visitor referred to the proceedings as a "multitude of bellowing mouths," and another called them "ignorant fanaticism."

Clergymen who saw their flocks being proselyted away to rival churches became critical. One stated that the whole plan was dishonest because it urged people to come to camp meetings to get religion, "when what they really wanted was a new crop of Methodists." Another said that they "produce effects on our intellectual and moral nature analogous to strong drink." And "it was almost as if conversion was an endurance contest; if the applicant could pass through the prescribed course of excitement, fear, distress, falling down, and then could compose himself, he considered himself converted."

Not all revivals were crude

Though much criticism against the camp meetings was justified, they rose and flourished in response to the spiritual and social poverty of the frontier. Visitors from the cultured centers of Europe were hardly qualified to view the revivals with clear understanding and without bias. Compared to their countries, the frontier was a boisterous, awkward, blundering adolescent, not sure of itself, and possessed with more energy than it knew what to do with.

Social activities of the camp meetings were by no means limited to courting and sex. It was *the* social event on the frontier, a holiday season, a time to "git acquainted," to escape from the humdrum monotony and drudgery of the isolated farms, an occasion to gossip and catch up with one's neighbors on what was going on in the world. It was a chance for "pleasurin'" for those with the "lone" sickness.

A number of observers stated that the social effects were good for women: "Many go home better than they came; even delicate women, who rarely step off a carpet for twelve months, grow more healthy from that time."

At the camp meeting no class distinction was recognized. All social groups were represented, men and women, young and old, all moving to the common rhythm of sin and salvation, for a brief season forgetful of political and economic rivalries, satisfied to be simply human. The camp meeting was "the perfect symbol of the motley, mongrel, praying, and laughing American democracy."[26]

The democratic feeling was declared in a camp meeting ditty:

> *Come hungry, come thirsty, come ragged, come bare,*
> *Come filthy, come lousy, come just as you are.*

One observer summed up the lure of the woodland gatherings as: "The love of variety and novelty—the desire for excitement—romantic feelings . . . love of good fellowship—and even a willingness to obtain cheap religious character. . . ."[27]

Not all the revivals were crude. And many described as crude must have had their finer, peaceful moments. Moore and Foster wrote of one in Tennessee: "At night the grove was illuminated with lighted candles, lamps and torches . . . The stillness of the night, the serenity of the heavens, the vast crowd of worshippers wrapped in a deep solemnity which covered every countenance, the pointed and earnest manner in which the preachers exhorted the people to repentance, faith and prayer . . . produced . . . solemn sensations in the minds of all."[28]

The best of them met the needs of the isolated woodland homes and the struggling primitive villages for some type of contact with a larger life and fuller interest than were afforded by their provincial daily existence. Men doubtless derived a mystical sense of communion with God and their fellow men that gave a renewed meaning and dignity to their lives. For a few days or a few weeks, human equality and solidarity became real in the camp meetings. The experience was not wholly forgotten when men returned to the more commonplace necessities of competitive living.[29]

Defenders of the institution declared that converts in those days were born strong into the kingdom, and entered it shouting, that in this experience of being "born strong" the agonizing body-shaking spiritual pangs of birth were followed by the feelings of joy and relief. The new child of God, they explained, at that moment of "self-surrender," instead of being gripped by tension and fear, entered into a state of peace and security and felt very close to heaven. The theologians believed that at this point the Holy Spirit entered and made a new creature of the sinner.

Many modern psychologists take the position that the violent body agitations at the camp meetings were not the manifestations of true religion, but the results of nervous instability, pathological emotionalism, and the deadening of rationality. These scientists coldly attribute the relief from these emotional storms, in seemingly odd manifestations, as nervous exhaustion, the only recourse left.

Though conversions "did not always stick," church membership rose as a result of the camp meeting as never before. A clergyman in 1840 estimated that nearly one half of the members of the Methodist Episcopal church "are the fruits of the camp meetings, directly or remotely." Church statistics reveal that membership of other Protestant denominations also increased by leaps and bounds (no pun intended).

Whatever the total results of the camp meetings, they were inspired by good motives, and prompted by men and women trying, as best they knew how, with their limited facilities, to find a better way of life, and bring godliness, as they understood it, to this earth in greater abundance.

VIII

CHURCH DISCIPLINE BEFORE COURT DISCIPLINE

Many people who came into the fold under the shouting, hell-fire preaching of the camp meeting evangelists found themselves more confused than consoled or informed once they left the thundering fright of the revival. With evangelical strategy designed to literally scare the devil out of the sinner, and with theology and doctrine neglected to a minimum, many converts were not sure just what the will of God was, as applied to their daily living. They found that they could not, day by day, live up to the high emotional pitch that had originally led them down the aisle to the altar. They had stood up for Jesus while the shouting and singing rang loudly and hell seemed close enough to scorch their eyebrows, but once back to the humdrum, exasperating tasks of their cabins and fields, they often found themselves on wobbly spiritual feet.

If the saints had come "rejoicing bringing in the sheaves," they pretty well had their work cut out for them once the shouting was over and the evangelical artillery moved on. If the frontier folk were capable of taking their religion in quick pungent doses, many were capable of losing it just as quickly. Thus, the church had much shepherding to do to keep the hastily corralled sheep from wandering from the fold before they could develop in the forest vineyards.

Fervent and persistent as the converting efforts were, the veterans were just as determined to keep the recruits on the straight and narrow once the evangelists had pointed them in the right direction.

The church exerted such effective discipline that it had far-reaching influence on the morals of the frontier at a time when virtually no other organized restraining force existed. Discipline of the church, as a rule, preceded that of the courthouse. The law of God in many regions was the regulator of society and business before legislatures and grand juries prevailed. The Scriptures stood as the statutes of the land, the church building the Lord's courthouse, the clergy served much as judges on the bench directing proceedings, with the deacons and elders frequently serving in a fashion as prosecuting and defending counsels, and the church membership sitting as a jury. Though church proceedings were less formal than those of the courthouse, they were none the less grave and somber.

Church discipline, though more democratic than secular discipline, was more strict, its watchfulness more constant and thorough. No act, from the market place to the boudoir, escaped the church's concern. And church action was quicker than court trials. The church membership could assemble and dispense immediate judgment.

Furthermore, the church expected members to act as their own "arresting officers." It was the duty of any member, if "guilty of public offense," to "come forward and make acknowledgement to the church without being sent for."[1]

No excuse for nonattendance

Nonattendance at church caused much disciplinary action. The very least expected of a member was regular church attendance. As a rule, the church brooked no excuse for non-attendance from a healthy man—long distances, poor roads, and slow transportation notwithstanding. Minutes of business meetings contain many accounts of warnings and exclusions for "failing to fill their seats," and "long absence from his seat." One church regarded absence of two Sundays as adequate reason for dealing with faltering members.

Improper and uncontrolled talk brought many members before church councils. With every brother's ear a potential espionage sounding post, members had to maintain a controlled tongue to keep their standing in the church and community. Church minutes reveal such charges as "improperly talking," "unsavory language," "hard sayings," and "unworldly conversation in the churchyards before and after the sermon."[2]

One sister was excluded "for frequently giving her mother the lie, & calling her a fool and Indeavouring by tattling to set several of the Neighbors at strife with each other."[3] One member was cited for making "illnatured expressions" and saying of a brother that he had no more fellowship for him than he had for the devil.[4] One Kentucky Baptist church gravely asked for instruction from its association about "what shall be done with members that are old and in their dotage and use impious language?"

A church member needed evidence to back up what he said if it was open to question. The church excluded many members "for telling lies." It excluded one member "for pushing a man in a dispute and giving him the lie in his own house," another for "lying, tattling and unguarded conversation."

Telling tall tales was risky business. One Peter Bruner reputedly said that in girting his saddle his hand slipped and struck him in the eye and "burst the ball out on his cheek and that he set it back with his hand." Either Brother Bruner was misquoted, or he thought better of his story once the church council made a point of it. He denied "saying so."

The denial was sustained, and Brother Bruner was "acquitted of the statement."[5]

But all bearers of extraordinary "tales" did not fare so fortunately in being interrogated by so trusting a congregation as Peter Bruner faced. The story is told about a Hard-Shell Baptist returning to his community after visiting Jefferson, Texas, and reporting to his neighbors that he had seen ice made there in July. (It is claimed that the first artificial ice in the United States was made at Jefferson.)

The church promptly charged the traveling brother with lying. But before expelling him, a member suggested that, in fairness to him, they should make an investigation. So the deliberating body appointed the brother making the suggestion to go to Jefferson and investigate.

He made the journey, and on his return reported that, amazing as it sounded, he actually saw ice made there with the temperature nearly a hundred in the shade.

The church turned both members out for lying.

A little cussin'

Church councils considered cursing and swearing among the worst "uses of the tongue." On the frontier "profanity was general and emphatic,"[6] and many were required to give account for their profane utterances.

One communicant brought before a discipline committee, pleaded that he did not think it possible to work oxen successfully in a stumpy, muddy country without "doing a little cussin'." They understood it and expected it, he insisted. The committee, which regarded the errant ox driver as an otherwise pious brother, and possibly in view of their firsthand knowledge of the stubborn nature of oxen, agreed to bear with him.

But church minutes reveal many quick expulsions for "vainly swearing," for "swearing & keeping another Man besides her Husband," for "swearing & wishing God might damn him if he did not kill his brother Richard. . . ."[7]

This account, though not documented, has persisted in the frontier country. A Negro deacon was up before the church for cursing. A fellow member related the circumstance.

The brethren were holding a wake at the church for old Uncle Mose. Now it so happened that Uncle Mose was extremely stooped. And consequently when he was placed in his coffin the lid had to be sprung down upon the corpse in order that it could be contained. Late that night some relatives of the deceased arrived at the church and wanted a last look at Uncle Mose. .And so the coffin lid was lifted for a view. But at that moment when the lid released the pressure from the artificially straightened body, Uncle Mose sprang up in his coffin.

"Now what does that have to do with Deacon Jones cussin'?" the preacher asked the testifying member.

"Well, about a minute after the coffin was open, Deacon Jones passed me a mile down the road. And when he went by he say: 'Damn a church ain't got but one door in it.' "

Drinking wasn't always sin

Nothing caused so much turmoil and dissension in the church, first and last, as drinking. In the early days of the frontier the making of whiskey was commonplace, and it was considered a staple. Preachers who objected to alcohol were the exception rather than the rule. John Wesley, though not an advocate of whiskey, advised his Methodist circuit riders to take "a little lemonade, mild ale, or candied orange peel."

Peter Cartwright, one of the most influential of the circuit riders, gave this testimony on the prevalence of liquor drinking on the frontier: "From my earliest recollection drinking drams, in family and social circles, was considered harmless and allowable socialities. It was almost universally the custom for preachers, in common with all others, to take drams; and if a man would not have it in his family, his harvest, his house-raisings, log-rollings, weddings, and so on, he was considered parsimonious and unsociable, and many, even professors of Christianity, would not help a man if he did not have spirits and treat the company."[8]

James B. Finley, another noted circuit rider, wrote in his autobiography: "Ardent spirits were used as a preventitive of disease. It was also regarded as a necessary beverage. A house could not be raised, a field of wheat could not be cut down, nor could there be a log-rolling, a husking, a quilting, a wedding, or a funeral without the aid of alcohol."[9]

Even the Baptists, who later went all out against liquor, apparently were not against it in the beginning. Early Baptist preachers were sometimes paid in barrels of whiskey.[10]

John James, a missionary among the Choctaw Indians, related this experience of his youth: "Accepting an invitation from Andrew Mann, a young man of my age, I accompanied him to his father's house nearby for dinner and found all the preachers there. Well do I remember, when Mrs. Mann called dinner that Elder Joseph Parker went out to his buggy and brought in a bottle of whiskey and set it on the table. After grace had been said by him, he passed the bottle around, as iced tea would now be passed, that is without excuse, and with as little harm, as none drank to excess."[11]

Apparently liquor attacked the preachers first, and they gradually retaliated. Certainly there must be many explanations for this turn against liquor by church people. But one fact is obvious: the frontier drunk became' a thorn in the side of the clergymen, for a favorite sport of the inebriated fun-seeking frontiersman was to try to break up church meetings. The sight of a straight-laced formal church congregation to a relaxed imbiber tended to inspire unrestrained hilarity.

It appears that the Hard-Shell Baptists were among the last to take up the fight against liquor—if the following anecdote is representative:

A traveler called at eventide at a farmhouse and requested

lodging for the night. The farmer was away. And so the housewife, being alone with her daughter, refused to take him in.

Then he asked: "How far is it to where a preacher can get lodging?"

"Oh, if you are a preacher, you can stay here," the housewife answered.

The preacher deposited his saddlebags in the house, and when he led his horse away to the barn, the mother and daughter began debating about what kind of preacher he was.

"He cannot be a Presbyterian," said one, "for he is not dressed well enough."

"He's not a Methodist," said the other, "for his coat is not cut right for a Methodist."

The daughter said: "If I could find his hymn book I could tell what kind of preacher he is."

And with that she stuck her hand into the saddlebags and, pulling out a flask of liquor, exclaimed: "La, Ma, he's a Hard-Shell Baptist."[12]

Once the pulpit took up the fight against alcohol, the movement waxed intense and unrelenting on a broad front until "Demon Rum" was denounced from the pulpit with much the same contempt normally reserved for the devil.

This about-face appears something of a paradox. Perhaps Archie Robertson came about as near as anyone getting to the heart of it when he said: "The fact is that we are an intemperate people, immoderately drunk or dry."[13]

The unsettled nature of the frontier accounts in some part for this unique campaign against liquor. In developed sections of the world, society was better organized, and effective law enforcement protected the church and its ministers against disturbances. But in the wilderness, where society had not taken root, and was still fluid and unrestrained by agencies of law, the church was faced with the basic task of protecting itself for survival and self-respect. It set out to do for itself what others would not or could not do for it. Moreover, on this money-scarce frontier liquor was draining off much of the money not used for the necessities of life. This slowed development, including that of the church.

Following the clergy, the first among the laity to take up the banner of abstinence were the women, individually and then in organized crusades. Few took the arduous action of Carry Nation and resorted to the hatchet, but many who had had difficulty keeping the pot boiling because the saloon-keeper beat the groceryman to the family wages became wandering, dedicated missionaries pleading for sobriety.

In time, the Woman's Christian Temperance Union was organized. The dry movement then took on numerous ramifications, particularly in politics. The movement was associated with, in order, the woman's rights movement resulting in woman suffrage, national prohibition, and the rise of gangsterism. Political parties were formed based on the issue, and in many sections, to this day, the lines are more closely drawn between Wets and Drys than between the Republicans and the Democrats.

At first the church congregations were inclined to bear with members whose thirst had been too much for them. It was the practice in many churches to administer correction which consisted in an acknowledgement of intemperance by the accused, whereupon the congregation would vote that the accused was censorable. Many churches would bear with members if it appeared they "were deceived or taken in," or if they promised "with the help of God to abstain for the future." There is record of one brother's bringing a complaint against himself. He expressed sorrow for his sin and stated that the Lord had pardoned him. The church followed the stated example of the Lord and permitted him to remain in fellowship.

As time went on, churches took an increasingly firm stand on drinking. Church minutes reveal expulsions for "drinking to excess," "for having been repeatedly Intoxicated with spiritous liquors," "for parting with his wife, getting drunk and dancing," "for drinking to excess and offering to fight."[14] Whiskey was responsible for the short duration of some memberships. For example, the minutes of one church reveal that "Elder R. G. Green joined by letter December 1838, and was excluded for drunkenness in February 1840."[15]

The Wets did not cork their bottles just because of the blast from the pulpit or the march of the "petticoat brigades," though none could ignore the concerted attempt to "dry up the country." About as much as they could do was to serve as examples for their cause, vote for it, and make jokes about the opposition.

For example, it was said of one candidate for political office that he would "belly up to the church and back up to the bar."

The drinking fraternity also enjoyed telling a story about a pious sister of the Anti-Saloon League who accosted a wobbly cowboy on the street, well along in his cups: "What are you going to do when you approach the Lord with whiskey on your breath?" she demanded, pointing a long finger under his nose.

The cowboy steadied himself for a moment, then said: "Lady, when I approach the Lord, I'm going to leave my breath here."[16]

The imbibers had their laughs, but it became increasingly evident that the church's crusade against liquor was no joke.

The evil of dancing

Next to drinking, dancing got more members excluded than anything else. Church minutes record many cases of expulsion for dancing and "permitting dancing in their home." Some people made it a habit to "dance out of the church" in the winter and be "saved" at the camp meeting the following summer when dancing was not in vogue.

Ministers not only denounced dancing from the pulpit, many declared it a sign of low morals in general. One wrote in his autobiography: "Men may say in admiration, 'That lady dances gracefully,' but it is at the expense of her virtue. It [the dance] brings up in gloomy array the smouldering virtue of too many thousands who have gone down under its perverting influences . . . How ruinous is this popular and enchanting evil!" He speaks of dancers as "victims of the night . . . enough to chill with horror . . . It is the dark sneak that legalizes a liberty between the sexes." In less than two pages he tells of half-a-dozen killings growing out of "dancing-parties."[17]

Just to be associated with dancing was enough to put one's Christianity under a cloud. Fiddlers were stigmatized by a common simile: "Thick as fiddlers in hell." Many church minutes show exclusions for "fiddling."

Actually, it appears that the side effects of dancing gave the pious more concern than dancing itself. They regarded it as the root of numerous social evils. By outlawing dancing they thought they might nip these evils in the bud.

It seems that almost anything could happen at a dance. Socially starved young people with pent-up emotions, often overcoming shyness with whiskey, and embarrassed by lack of education and culture, often fell victim to misunderstandings and assumed affronts. The backwoods produced a touchy, hair-trigger breed.

Fights at dances were common. A notorious "dance fight" started when one cowboy said to another cowboy that his girl friend danced like a zephyr. The cowboy resented the remark, and set out in a flash to defend his girl's honor. In the melee a lady was pushed over, the dogs in the yard became excited and ran about barking, which in turn startled the horses, with the result that two teams ran away with surreys, completely wrecking one.

Only after the defendant of his girl's honor had fought himself into bloody and bruised exhaustion did it come out that he thought the other cowboy had said his girl danced like a heifer.

Whatever the basic cause of trouble at dances the church member usually had to answer to a concerned congregation for his "wayward" actions.

Though dances afforded convenient meeting places for high-tempered people on the frontier where fists settled more arguments than reason, almost any gathering place might provide a circumstance for "disorderly conduct" worthy of church attention. Church minutes abound with such charges as "overtaken in a passion," "disturbing the peace," "striking his brother," "fighting his wife," etc. Usually the church was successful in bringing the antagonists together, and seeing peace between them reached, and agreeing to bear with them.

She wasn't fanatic about being a virgin

Improper relations between the sexes resulted in numerous charges. The Glen's Creek (Kentucky) Church considered three charges of adultery on one day, and the "Sharon (Kentucky) Church excluded on similar charges two offenders at one meeting."[18]

"Sister Woolridge's Saunders," the records of one church reveals, "was brought again before the church for leaving the wife he had when he joined the Church & taking Rachel from another man and living in Adultery with her. . . ."[19]

The Forks of Elkhorn (Kentucky) Baptist Church "excluded Charles a Negro Man belonging to Br. Majors for busing Winney a black member belonging to Sister Boulware." This church excluded a member "for lying, & taking another wife contrary to the gospel." It also brought a charge against "Clary a black woman of Bro. Edm. Ware's for being too intimate & sleeping with Joe a Man of Capt. Taylors. . . ."[20]

Minutes of the Wood River Baptist Church, Illinois, September 1, 1820, carried this report: "We a committee appointed to enquire into the conduct of br John Conner and

Sister Molly blak people and do find from examination and from their own confession that br Conner is guilty of falsehood in denying that he had ever tried Sister Molly to sleep with her and after confessing that he had tried her for the purpose of proving whether she was a bad woman or not and charge Sister Molly with agreeing to quit her husband and take br Conner."[21]

Sometimes members were apparent victims of gossip. The church investigated, and when sufficient evidence favored the accused the church received him back or continued him in fellowship, as the case might be. "The matter of Thos Musick taken up & it is the opinion of this Assn that he ought to be taken into fellowship of this body of Baptist & that if in future any further testimony shall be fowarded to convince us that he is guilty of fornication they are to give him up to be as he was before, for we believe the testimony of Margaret Bridges not sufficient to exclude him."[22]

The church usually took as proof of guilt failure of a member to answer a charge. It charged David Allen of Glen's Creek (Kentucky) Church with making "an unlawful attempt to go to bed with" the wife of another member of the church. It summoned him to meet his accuser in a church trial. He did not appear, and the assembly excluded him immediately.

Detailed church records lead one to believe that just about everything the lusty frontier people did, the church found out about it sooner or later. The minutes of the Cooper Run (Kentucky) Church carries an account of the "disgraceful" doings of a "married vamp" who permitted a young man to "kiss her three times." John Carlisle of the Cahawaba (Alabama) Church was expelled for "trying to kiss a young woman." Two girls were each charged with "having a little one."

Minutes of the Methodist Annual Conference held in Circleville, Ohio, in 1834 reveal that Robert Graham was charged with the "hugging of two different women—kissing them." He denied that he hugged them, but "owned that he had lain his arm about one." He was expelled.

John McKearn, a Presbyterian of the Missouri Territory, faced the charge "that he sat down on a pallet besides her (a member of the church) and laid his head upon her feet and clasped her legs in his arms." At a wake he reportedly was seen "with his right arm across her legs," and later "with his head reclining upon her lap." The church concluded that he "had designs of seduction" and suspended him from all church privileges.

It appears that under some circumstances the ignorant accused members did not fully understand the language that church propriety required, and may not have represented themselves to best advantage. This illustrative story is told of a Negro girl who, accused of improper relations with the opposite sex, was brought before a church assembly and thought by the examiner to be either quibbling or without clear understanding of the charges against her. Finally he asked her the direct question: "Are you a virgin?"

Without hesitation the girl replied: "Yessuh, I is." Then she hesitated in thoughtful meditation for a moment, and added emphatically: "But I ain't no fanatic about it!"

They weren't meek about it

All members did not submit meekly to the church's jurisdiction. They considered it prying into their intimate, personal affairs. And they stood up and said so. It sometimes took as much courage on the part of a preacher to bring accused persons to trial as it did for frontier peace officers to apprehend and secure convictions for outlaws. Many of the preachers were just as tough as the peace officers. The case of L. M. White will illustrate:

White, according to his own statement, was before his conversion guilty of social and moral outlawry. He "drank,

gambled, fought and caroused, caring for nothing or nobody."
He went to a camp meeting one night to find out, if possible,
how many indictments the last grand jury had returned
against him. He heard that there were some indictments
against him. But he also heard a sermon that converted him
on the spot.

White was never a man to dilly-dally. He said that God
had forgiven him. He began his ministry the next day. "I
saddled my horse, put two good Remington pistols in one
side of my saddlebags, and my Bible and hymn book in the
other. I needed the pistols as much as my Bible," he related.
The conference had assigned him to an outlaw rendezvous.

The grand jury, as was usually the case, took the stand that
if God could forgive such a sinner, the state should follow
suit.

It was not long before White came face to face with the
leader of an outlaw band named Bill Hawkins he had ridden
with. Both men carried guns. Whether or not the outlaw had
any respect for the cloth, he had good reason to respect the
courage and marksmanship of his onetime saddle pal.

In the outlaw community a woman had left her husband
and was living with another man. White announced that the
woman would be tried in church. He summoned her to appear on a specified day to answer the charge of adultery.

Hawkins put out the word that if anyone said aught against
the woman he would be shot on the spot.

The entire community was terrified.

A steward pleaded with White not to try the woman. "Bill
Hawkins will kill somebody," he warned.

White told of the incident: "I told him [the steward] to
come on, that we were going to have the class meeting, and
we would turn that woman out. When I walked into the
church there sat Hawkins and some half dozen of his gang,
with red bandanas tied around their necks so in case shooting
began each fellow would know his pal. I walked to the table
and placed my Bible and hymn book thereon, and my two

Remingtons on either side. I looked Bill in the eye (I had soldiered with him) and said: 'Bill, I can't preach much, but I can shoot. That much you know. If you open your mouth or make a move at this meeting I aim to shoot you right between the eyes.' Roll call of members and character passed. Finally we reached the name of this woman. 'Does anyone know of any Christian misconduct by this woman?' was asked. No answer. I called on some brother to preside, and I picked up my pistols, and I charged the sister with adultery and moved that we exclude her from the communion and class. Got no second. I put the motion, voted aye, and as moderator declared her dismissed. Bill signaled his men and left."[23]

On the frontier godliness was never to be taken as a sign of weakness. Piousness may have motivated the bringing of religion to this region, but it often took unflinching toughness to make it stick.

Mrs. Weeks left her husband

The church kept a close eye to the keyhole for any trouble between married couples. Elijah Weeks and his wife were members of the Plum Creek (Kentucky) Church. Mrs. Weeks left her husband, and the church immediately made the separation its concern, without request from Weeks. After a hearing, the church instructed Weeks to take his wife back. He refused, and was promptly expelled.

In the case of a Negro couple, Jane and Simm, Jane was excluded because she refused to live with Simm, and Simm was excluded because he disagreed with Jane. Polly Speer was excluded for "having two husbands at one time."[24]

A Mississippi Presbyterian was churched because he "shoved his wife so that she fell across a chair and continued in that position for several minutes . . . he shoved her out of his house and shut the door against her."

The congregation of the Forks of Elkhorn (Kentucky)

Baptist Church discussed at length "whether it is lawful for a slave being an orderly member and compelled to leave his wife and move with his master about five hundred miles then to take another wife? . . . Debated and withdrawn."

The minutes of the Elkhorn (Kentucky) Baptist Association carried a query from the Marble Creek Church asking "whether a woman slave that left a husband in the old country and married again here to a man that has a wife twenty miles from him who . . . refuses to keep said man as a husband, ought her marrying in such circumstance be a bar to her membership." In accordance with the association's answer she was "debarred from membership."

Affairs of courtship, including the "intentions" of lovers, came under the surveillance of the church. The daughter of a member of the French Board (Tennessee) Baptist Church was courted by a young member from another church. The courtship came to a sudden end. A committee of six brethren, three from each church, took up the matter and rendered the unanimous opinion that the accused young man was guilty of "wilfully, wickedly, falsely, maliciously, deceitfully imposing himself on Brother ———, and his family, and particularly on his said daughter, by pretending a wish to marry her without any such intention." The church expelled the false lover.[25]

Some church deliberations divided members in their opinions, and decisions were reached with great difficulty. A young sister was caught in the act of hugging and kissing a gay young "sinner," and brought before the church. The evidence was conclusive. One of the leading sisters of the congregation had walked behind the young lovers on the way home from church, and had witnessed the disgraceful carryings-on.

Some members thought there might be extenuating circumstances, that the girl might not have been entirely to blame—it was spring, with moonlight and a shaded road, and the boy was very handsome.

The stricter faction, however, thought that such love-making was a disgrace, that if a stop was not put to it the country would go to the dogs.

Only after a long and heated discussion, when the members could not agree, they turned instinctively to the old grandmother of the church, whose long Christian life was beyond reproach, and asked her advice, saying they would abide by it.

She was reluctant. But finally she arose and rendered her opinion on the love-making. She said she believed that "if there was more of it done, and less said about it, the world would be better off."[26]

The church agreed to bear with the "misled" young woman.

The many uses of tobacco

Tobacco was condemned from some pulpits. But its use was so general in the backwoods with both men and women that all the preaching made but slight dent on the practice. It served a multitude of purposes, perhaps, in part, because it was usually handy. It served in the home as an insecticide and as a medicine. Tobacco poultices were applied to wounds to stop bleeding and as a treatment for snakebite. Smoke was blown into ears to relieve earaches. Tobacco was said to be good for jaundice, dyspepsia, toothache, and for corpulent persons in that it would make them "spit their fat away." Some parents testified that unhealthy children began to grow when they started using tobacco. They theorized that the poison of the tobacco killed the poisons existing in their systems.[27]

It was a common saying that a cowboy out of tobacco was an individual not to be fooled with. One manager of the XIT Ranch ordered cigarette papers for his line riders by the carload.[28] A trail boss said he was afraid to let a cowboy out of tobacco carry a gun.

A housewife argued with her pastor that she just couldn't see how a woman could put out a big wash without a little snuff.

Even the hard-hitting evangelist, Sam Jones, did not go all out against tobacco. But to help the distressed women of a certain town save a new church carpet from tobacco juice, he had this to say at the beginning of a sermon: "I did not come here to deliver an anti-tobacco lecture, and if I had I wouldn't expect to get anywhere with a lot of old billy goats like you. I am not asking you to quit chewing tobacco, but you can do without it long enough to attend church.

"If you have got a fresh chew in your mouth when you get here and don't want to lose it, if that is the idea, just take it out of your mouth and put it on a chip and lay it outside the door step and you can get it when you get out of church. There isn't a dog in the world that would touch it; there isn't a hog in the universe that would come within ten feet of it if he knew what it was. But I'll tell you, Bud, you'd better mark your chip; some man might get it."[29]

On another occasion Jones said of an old hardened addict: "His idea of Heaven is an old slick stump to sit on and spit."[30]

"Dirty mouth" individuals were sometimes pointed out in the congregation. James Axley criticized a man in his audience for spitting "all over the floor" and referred to him as "that dirty, nasty, filthy tobacco-chewer, sitting on the end of that front seat."

The pastor of an Austin, Texas, church posted a placard over the church door with this message admonishing his congregation against tobacco chewing:

> *Ye chewers of that noxious weed*
> *Which grows on earth's most cursed sod*
> *Be pleased to clean your filthy mouths*
> *Outside the sacred House of God*

Throw out your "plug and cavendish"
Your "pig tail" "twist" and "honey dew"
And not presume to spit upon
The pulpit, aisles or in the pew.[31]

It was a practice in the heat of some revivals for men to throw their tobacco pouches away. But a common saying had it that the repentants usually remembered where they threw them.

Though preachers continually badgered members from the pulpit to give up their "unclean habit," this writer has seen no account of anyone chewing or smoking himself out of the church. The habit was too well rooted on the frontier before the preachers and the churches arrived.

The price of wild recreation

The church considered it its prerogative to regulate all affairs of society, including recreation. The frontier folk worked long and hard hours, and when rare moments of leisure came, they relaxed "hard." Recreation in the Wild West doubtless would have been much wilder but for the ever restraining hand of the church.

Church minutes record disciplinary action—for a father allowing his children to have "frolicking" at home, a sister for "joining in plays and pastimes at newyears," for a group of young people for "frivolity and riot" on the Fourth of July. (They were admonished to use that day for prayer and the reading of the Declaration of Independence.) Two members were excluded for "improper conduct in time of worship playing of ball."[32] One church passed a resolution "that it is not agreeable to the gospel for any of her members to attend on Barbeques."

Too much love for fast horses got many enthusiasts into church trouble. A council censored a member for going to a race track and holding the stakes while the horses ran. A camp meeting preacher said that "there is a class of people who can't go to hell fast enough on foot, so they get on their poor mean ponies and go to the horse race."[33]

The church delved into various minor infractions. Councils registered disapproval against elaborate funeral processions, jesting at the courthouse, short-haired women and long-haired men. Sam Jones, revealing that "God never intended a woman to be exposed in the eyes of the world," said in a revival sermon: "When a woman is vulgar enough to cut her dresses low-necked, she's not liable to get shocked at anything I say."[34]

Doctrines and Disciplines of the Methodist Episcopal Church, published in 1808, revealed a stand of this church against "brother going to law with brother," "use of many words in buying and selling," "speaking evil of magistrates or ministers," "the putting on of gold and costly apparel," "laying up of treasures on earth."

Social decorum came under the watchful eye of the church. Young ladies at Stewart Female Academy were constantly told that it was uncouth for a young lady to cross her legs. They were "constantly admonished to get the knots out of their lower extremities or to uncross their pedal extremities."

The same list of instructions stated that it was "not considered sinful to smile at a preacher's son." But students were instructed not to converse with persons on the street.[35]

Ministers, too, were disciplined

Ministers, as well as members, were disciplined—by their conferences, associations, and congregations. Some were removed from their assignments because of personality clashes. One was removed for argumentativeness, another for "worldliness," and one overeager minister for daring "to say the blessing for several meals in visiting homes without waiting for his superiors to arrive at the table." A quarterly conference in Georgia brought before it a minister to answer for ostentatious display in the wearing of "gold spectacles."

Some ministers did not make the transition to the new nondrinking code with sufficient dispatch to suit some of the "old-fashioned" congregations. Once a frontier church put the stamp of sin on an act, it brooked no dalliance.

A preacher, walking the straight and narrow route through dry territory, could not afford to be careless or clumsy for a moment. An apparent bit of awkwardness by the Reverend John Gillespie resulted in a trial that took up twelve pages in the minutes of the Shiloh Presbytery in Tennessee in 1821.

A witness testified before this church body that at a cornhusking the Reverend Gillespie "having been asked to serve the chicken was so intoxicated that he missed the chicken and stuck the fork into the table."

Apparently the church considered the minister's chicken-serving experience a mishap, for, after lengthy deliberation, it rendered a verdict of acquittal, and censored his accusers.

The Reverend William Mahan of the Transylvania Presbytery did not fare so well before a council on a charge of intoxication. A witness testified that he "smelled very strong of whiskey." Another witness stated that once when conducting family worship he "went to sleep while they were singing," and "once or twice slept a minute or two with the book in his hands" and "nodded once or twice during prayer."

The Reverend Mahan was expelled. He repeatedly petitioned the church for reinstatement, and was repeatedly refused. He turned to schoolteaching. Possibly the habit had already gripped him, or his frustration and disappointment drove him to the bottle for relief, for an ex-student later described him as "an able teacher and a drunken preacher."[36]

Some ministers were accused of too much familiarity with the opposite sex. The Reverend Jeremiah Abell was brought before the Ebenezer Church of the Transylvania Presbytery in November 1824 to face such a charge. Mrs. Annas Buchanan testified to the effect that in the month of June or July "she was at her brother Saml Cauldwell [his home], that she slept in the room with her bro. and his wife and children, that Mr. Abell lodged in the same room, that in the night Mr. Abell came to her bed and awakened her by inviting her in a whisper to go to the kitchen to smoke. She refused audibly . . . He then made some forcible essays to excite her passions by thrusting his hands into her busom and approaching parts peculiarly feminine, that after passing an hour at least in these indecencies he retired, that in the morning between break of day and sunrise she was awakened by pressure of his hands in her busom; that he continued for some time making his attempts as before until as she supposed he saw or heard her brother coming into the room. . . ."

A Mrs. Martin Scott testified that "on or about the 22 of November, 1823, Mr. Abell called at the house of her husband, that after the usual civilities he inquired if she was alone, she said that she was but expected her mother soon, that she invited him to sit down which he refused to do unless she would sit on his knee, that she objected to sitting on his lap and said she would sit on a chair, that he still insisted and drew her to him, that during the time she was sitting in this position, which was, she believed, ten or fifteen minutes, he hugged and kissed her, that his conversation during the time was that of strong affection, saying he loved her as a child, had the same anxiety for her temporal and spiritual welfare as that of his own children, that he cautioned her against letting the world know his conduct saying it would not do to let the world know how intimate he was with his sisters, that she often attempted to rise and that Mr. Abell urged her to sit still, slightly holding her and saying it was more pleasant to be with her than to ride the lonesome road to Marrowbone. . . ."

Mrs. Sally Johnston "being qualified deposed and said that Mr. Abell came home from preaching after her husband who had invited him, that the next morning early he wished his horse to start home, that while her husband went for his horse Mr. Abell came to her bed and put his hand into her busom, that she expelled his hand by drawing the bed clothing more closely over her, that he left her bed, supposing, as the witness thinks, that he heard footsteps, that he again returned and was there until footsteps were heard or supposed to be heard, that upon her husband entering the house he took a chair and sat by the bed and played with her children."

Abell was "suspended from the exercise of the office of the gospel ministry until restored by an act of the Presbytery."

At Danville, April 29, 1825, the church "Resolved that the sentence of suspension passed on Mr. Abell be and it is hereby removed and he is restored to the full exercise of the office of the gospel ministry."[37]

William Warren Sweet comments in this connection that "the early restoration of Mr. Abell to the full exercise of the privilege of the gospel ministry, after he had been suspended for immorality, is a commentary on the liberal attitude of the frontier on matters of sexual morality."[38]

Attending circuses was a serious offense in the eyes of some churchmen. Bishop E. M. Marvin wrote of this practice in a letter, about the year 1870:

"I have encountered one thing here which I believe is without precedent in the history of traveling preachers. Two members of the conference have been to the circus. I write this in hesitation. But it is a *fact*. Indeed, one of them was quite an old minister, a man of high standing. I was amazed. The fact is, there has been a good deal of looseness in this particular. The members, and perhaps local preachers, had been attending circuses in this country with impunity, until the demoralization had reached the pitch indicated in the fact which I have named. The conference did what seemed to it necessary to recover the church from this malady of worldliness. It was sad to see a man of grey hairs called to account in the conference for going to a circus. But the deed has been done and the conference could not overlook so grave an irregularity. I hope never . . . to hear of another Methodist pastor so far forgetting all the proprieties of his character and position."[39]

Some preachers stood up firmly and defended themselves in the face of congregational charges—and won. One pastor labored six days for his flock, but early every Saturday morning he went fishing and spent the day at it.

Called to account for his idleness, he was asked: "How can you waste a whole day every week fishing when Satan's so busy in this community. He certainly doesn't take any time off!"

"I don't suppose he does," the pastor agreed. "But I'm not following *his* example."

And he kept right on fishing and preaching in the same community.

Even the most prominent of the stalwarts, on occasion, found themselves defendants before church councils. Sometimes preacher was pitted against preacher. A stormy trial occurred at the Illinois Annual Methodist Conference in 1857 as a result of the Reverend Daniel J. Snow accusing Peter Cartwright of "being responsible for his being made an assistant pastor," and calling another minister "a damned son of a Bitch."[40]

It was one man's word against another. And, in the end, the charges against Cartwright were not sustained.

Some councils took ingenious means to prevent pastors from "out-Scripturing" them and taking detours from the exemplary path. A Negro pastor was found embracing one of the sisters of the congregation. When summoned before the church to answer for his actions, he defended himself with Scripture: "Doan it say in de Book dat de shepherd taketh de lamb unto his busom?" The committee deliberated, and then passed the following resolution: "Be it resolved that we keep Brother Jones as pastor, but that in the future, when he taketh a lamb unto his busom, it shall be a ram lamb."

Being a member of the church on the frontier was a serious and grave matter.

One thing is certain—during this plastic age of the West, when it was virtually without institutions of culture, learning, or law enforcement, and morals were at a low ebb, the church served as a vital stabilizing force. Its influence in elevating the morals of the country was tremendous.

IX

RIVALRY AMONG DENOMINATIONS

Denominational rivalry waxed strong on the frontier. The surging vigor of the new land demanded something more exciting and alive and personal, even in religion, than formality. Mere existence for the pioneers was something of a contest. One circumstance or another, or a combination of circumstances, cast most of them on definite sides—whites against Indians, aristocrats against the common folk, squatters versus ranchers, sheepmen versus cattlemen, Drys versus Wets, Protestants versus Catholics, Methodists versus Baptists, etc.

Isolation, lack of learning, communication and common cultural interests tended to breed narrow-mindedness and partisanship. Few neutrals existed on the frontier.

Much of the denominational bickering seems amusing now. But whatever the pioneer believed, he usually believed with the emotional tenacity common to ignorance and prejudice, and he expressed himself accordingly.

Though many of the spiritual darts cast were outwardly good-natured and in the manner of backwoods hurrahing, the undercurrent was more often dead-serious. Many of the frontier people believed that there was only one route to the Glory Land—and pride and vanity and narrow-mindedness usually convinced the spiritual traveler that only he and his caravan possessed the correct road map.

Politics caused one of the first serious religious conflicts. When the Anglo-Saxon immigrants went to Spanish Texas under the leadership of Stephen F. Austin they found the Catholic church the government-established religion. Austin, in the beginning, expressed more interest in securing freedom of land for the colonists than freedom of religion. But fiery missionaries considered the home hereafter more important than any earthly home in Texas. Political expediency designed to secure the free land Austin had in mind for temporal homes hardly seemed to them vital enough to justify tampering with the route to the Promised Land they were boosting.

Austin found it difficult to prevent the "noisy Methodists" from upsetting his political applecart. On January 1, 1824, he wrote: "There are two obstacles which hinder immigration to this province: One is the doubt which exists concerning slavery and the other religion."[1] In February 1829 he wrote: ". . . in some instances they [the Methodists] are too fanatic, too violent and too noisy . . . I assure you it will not do to have the Methodist excitement raised in this country."[2]

Austin pleaded for patience on the part of the Protestant colonists. But the preachers refused to hold their tongues. When he did not support them, many turned against him, as this letter of Austin reveals: "The Methodists have raised the cry against me, this is what I wished for if they are kept out, or will remain quiet if here for a short time we shall succeed in getting a free toleration of all Religions, but a few fanatics and imprudent preachers at this time would ruin us— We must show the government that we are ready to submit to their laws and willing to do so. After that we can, with some certainty of success, hope to have our privileges extended."[3]

To secure his colony, Austin was forced, in time, to take

firm measures. He wrote that the nation had finally settled down with a constitution modeled after that of the United States with the exception that the Catholic religion was exclusive, that this was the law of the land "and as such must be obeyed. And if a Methodist, or any other preacher except a Catholic, was to go through this country preaching I shall be compelled to imprison him. All the children in the country must be baptized in the Roman Church, and all the marriages celebrated in that church. This is the law. . . ."[4]

But law or no law, neither Austin nor the Mexicans could stand up against the Protestant "noise." The preachers continued it, and though they did not "right" the situation via the pulpit, they never let up until it was drowned in the roar of cannon, and religious freedom was established under the Lone Star, and in time further secured under the Stars and Stripes. It takes little imagination to reckon the part the "noisy" preachers played in bringing religious freedom to this part of the frontier. Many of them shouldered rifles and backed their words with gunpowder during the Texas Revolution. Such "noise" had now helped push religious freedom from the Atlantic Coast to the Rio Grande.

John the Baptist and John the Methodist

The frontier preachers girded themselves for a fight for their cause, whatever they considered it to be—and they were an unwavering and dedicated lot. When they had time off from fighting the devil they often used it to throw verbal punches at each other.

The Methodists and the Baptists were the strongest rivals on the frontier. They locked spiritual horns at the very beginning.

Denominational enthusiasts wrote "pep" songs. The Baptists sang one which ran:

> *Baptist, Baptist, Baptist,*
> *Baptist till I die.*
> *I'll go along with the Baptists*
> *And eat that Baptist pie.*

The Methodists had a reply in song:

> *The world, the devil and Tom Paine*
> *Have tried their force, but all in vain,*
> *They can't prevail, the reason is*
> *The Lord defends the Methodists.*[5]

The Baptists regarded the Methodists as the most persistent proselytizers. The determined Methodist circuit rider gave rise, among Baptists, to a description of the worst possible weather: "There's nobody out today but crows and Methodist preachers."

The Methodist circuit rider did not wait for a church to be built to commence preaching. He preached in homes or wherever he could attract listeners. Thus he inspired jealousy in other sectarians when they went into what they thought was virgin territory and found that they had been preceded by him. So, with more jealousy than malice, the saying became common that "the Methodist preacher is far in advance of even the Yankee Clock Peddler."[6]

Some Baptists made sport of the emotionalism and display of the Methodists. One instance exasperated Peter Cartwright no end—probably because of his helplessness under the circumstance. A young daughter of a Baptist preacher made a practice of saying when one of his converts "would fall under the power of God" that "it was nothing but a Methodist fit."[7]

Logic took some odd twists in frontier arguments. Some arguments ranged to the absurd. But they nonetheless impressed partisans on the frontier, where a laugh at the other denomination's expense was regarded as a victory of sorts.

Frederick L. Olmsted, told of an old Negro settler, the

only Baptist in his neighborhood, sticking up for his religion:

"You kin read, now, kean't you?"

"Yes."

"You read 'bout John de Baptist, hain't you?"

"Yes."

"Well, you never read 'bout any John de Methodist."[8]

Here is another much enjoyed Negro story which illustrates the predominating strength of "humor" over logic in frontier religious disputation.

An old Negro, a member of the Baptist Church, was given a litter of puppies by a Methodist neighbor. Before he left with them the Methodist minister appeared, and to make conversation with the new owner of the puppies, he asked: "What denomination are they?"

In respect to the Methodist donor, who was present, he answered: "Dey's Methodist dogs."

A week later the preacher chanced by the Negro's place, and seeing the puppies running about in the yard asked him again what denomination they belonged to.

"Dey's Baptist dogs."

"But you told me last week they were Methodist pups."

"But dey didn't have dar eyes open den."

Methodists early showed equal adeptness at playing up what they considered weaknesses in the Baptist armor.

In 1768 in Spotsylvania County, Virginia, they effected the arrest of five Baptist preachers for disturbing the peace, charging that "they cannot meet a man upon the road but that they must ram a text of Scripture down his throat."[9]

The Methodists, who boasted of some margin of learning over the Baptists (though hardly enough, it would seem, to boast about), took digs at their ignorance. They gave one definition of a Methodist as "a Baptist who has learned to read and write."

James H. Addison wrote of victory over the Baptists and the devil: "Methodism received a fresh impetus, and I think it is so well established that nothing can move it now. The combined powers of the Baptists and the Devil will be unavailing towards shaking the fabric thus reared."[10]

One booster attempted to show the superior qualities of Methodism by associating it with the attractive features of the state of Texas, describing the region as "a great, beautiful, dry weather, cotton, cattle, Methodist, liveoak state."[11]

Even in their discouragements, the Methodists frequently tossed barbs at their rivals. A circuit rider, lamenting upon the discouraging spiritual results in his district, wrote that he traveled three fourths of the way around his circuit and found "nothing cheering, or encouraging, many of the members have backslidden and are spiritually dead—some have gone to dancing schools and some have joined the Baptists."[12]

Sprinkling or immersion

The most heated and persistent disputes arose over the ordinance of baptism.

Peter Cartwright, a member of a "sprinkling denomination," said of the Baptists: "Indeed, they make so much ado about baptism by immersion, that the uninformed would suppose that heaven was an island, and there was no way to get there but by diving or swimming . . . They adopted the mode of immersion, the water-god of all exclusive errorists." He said that Baptist preachers "generally sang their sermons, and when they struck the long roll of their sing-song mode of preaching, in substance it was 'water,' 'water,' 'water.'"[13]

Methodist circuit rider Oscar M. Addison referred to the Baptists in his correspondence as the watery tribe and expressed resentment at their attempts to persuade "Methodists to join them and be Buried—alive!!" with water.[14]

The church records of a sprinkling denomination noted that a certain member had withdrawn "by being immersed into the Baptist Church."

The Baptists and Methodists often got on each other's nerves, even in little matters. James H. Addison wrote in January 1851 of an exasperating experience on his circuit where he spent the night with an old man "an 'Arkansawen' and an old Granny—the old lady a Baptist and an ignorant one at that, one that wants every body to 'follow the Lord down in the water'—The Lord save me from old Baptist women."[15]

A Methodist friend of Dr. J. B. Gambrell once said to him: "Doctor, you Baptists remind me of an ox on a hot day in July. Every time you see a little water, you run and jump into it."

Gambrell replied: "Yes, yes, my brother, and you Methodists remind me of a dog with hydrophobia. Every time you see a little water it throws you into a fit."[16]

A Baptist clergyman, conscious of a few Methodists in his congregation, gave an object lesson on the creation of the world: "God made the world, one-fourth land and three-fourths water, no doubt having baptism in view when he made it."[17]

A Baptist brother read from a Methodist hymnal which said: "We shall sail into the harbor on that day." He called this to the attention of a Methodist friend, and chided him: "I have often wondered how the Methodists ever hoped to get to heaven, but now I see they mean to use the water route on the home stretch."[18]

A sprinkling preacher, just returned from the Holy Land, announced in a sermon that he had visited the Jordan River where Christ was baptized and found "it so small a stream that a man could dam it up with his foot."

At this statement a Baptist in the congregation rose and said: "Mr. Preacher, I would give more to see that man's foot than I would to see the Jordan."[19]

One elderly Methodist sister had the shock of her religious life when her daughter joined the Baptist Church. She explained this "act of treason" of her erring daughter to her neighbors thus: "She's left the Army of the Lord and joined the Navy."

The Baptists never let up on criticism of infant baptism. A "declaration of open war" was declared between the Methodist and Baptist in Erath County, Texas, in July 1866. According to the Methodist account, the "opposing church" delivered a challenge "offering 500 head of cattle to anyone who could show infant baptism from the Scriptures." The Reverend Peter W. Graves accepted the challenge, and a bond was drawn up. The opposing preacher announced a day for the debate. And on that day a vast crowd assembled from far and near to witness the contest.

The Methodist historian Macum Phelan states that Graves spent two hours expounding his doctrine, and "before he was through he heard exclamations of despair among the opposition, some saying, 'The cattle are gone!'"

But Graves did not get the cattle, the Methodist explanation being that the opposition "smarted" him out of them, claiming that the bond was defective.

But once Graves had girded for battle and tasted victory, he set out to win further laurels for the cause of infant baptism. He decided to bring up the artillery while he considered the opposition in retreat. He enlisted the support of his presiding elder, James M. Johnson, and arranged a debate between him and "Choctaw Bill," a noted frontier preacher of "the opposing faith." Phelan indicates that the "war" brought a notable victory to Graves and the Methodists. He reported that "the other side was so badly routed that their church disbanded, and Methodism began to thrive in that country. Graves reported 100 conversions on his work at the close of the year."[20]

One Baptist preacher said of a sprinkler's preaching on infant baptism: "He goes to church and preaches about an hour and a half on infant baptism, when two-thirds of the men are going to hell, and all the babies are asleep."

The Presbyterians were more reserved about infant baptism than the Baptists and Methodists—at least they made less fuss about it. Some Presbyterians tried not to make a soul-shaking issue of it, and regardless of church doctrine and church loyalty spoke their individual feelings and sought their own route toward peace of mind—as revealed in a report sent to the Presbytery of Cincinnati concerning one of its members: ". . . he is of the opinion that the Baptists have more scripture for their views and practices in relation to infant baptism than Presbyterians have, and who moreover informed this brethren that he does not wish to hear anything more on the subject because when discussed it perplexes his mind and renders him uncomfortable."[21]

Falling from grace and backsliding

The sects disputed other doctrinal points, both privately and publicly. One of the most popular subjects of debate, second only to baptism, dealt with the difference between falling from grace and backsliding.

The repartee between Sam Jones, a Methodist of the belief that one might gain grace and then fall from it, and Dr. Rufus C. Burleson, a Baptist of the stand that once saved always saved, will illustrate:

Jones reportedly said to Dr. Burleson: "Bless you, you will soon be in heaven. You are ripening for glory . . . I want you to tell Jesus when you get there that Sam Jones is coming."

"I'm sorry, Sam, I can't do it," Burleson replied.

"Why can't you?" the surprised Methodist evangelist said.

"Well, you might fall from grace and go to hell, and I would be turned out of heaven for lying."[22]

A number of sects took the foot-washing practice, common in the sandal-wearing times of Jesus, literally as a religious ritual to be followed in imitation of the practice of Jesus. They regarded this ritual with the importance approaching that afforded to baptism, and observed it accordingly.

Some who did not regard ceremonial public foot washing as an inspired example to be followed, poked fun at the practice—as illustrated in the following story:

A zealous member of a foot-washing sect encountered an Episcopal bishop during a train journey and tried to engage him in conversation on doctrinal points.

The bishop, at the moment busily engaged in preparing a sermon and not wishing to get into an argument, attempted to brush the man off politely with a noncommittal remark.

The foot washer, not to be denied, decided to needle the bishop on his denomination's scant use of water, said pointedly: "We believe in foot washing in our church. Do you?"

"My dear sir," said the bishop looking up sternly from his unfinished sermon, "we not only believe in it, we insist upon it."

Sometimes ministers, particularly young ones, were not sure what stand they should take on doctrine and procedural differences among the various denominations. On the preacher-scarce frontier, so the story goes, a young Methodist minister found himself in a quandary when asked in an emergency to conduct a funeral for a Baptist. Not able to decide what to do, he wired his bishop for instructions.

The bishop wired back: "Bury all the Baptists you can."[23]

Campbellites, in time, became strong enough to inspire jealous concern among other denominations, particularly the Methodists.

The Reverend James H. Addison wrote of his frontier circuit, expressing the current Methodist point of view: "Here . . . the prowling wolves of Campbellism, Drunkardism, and Devilism of every grade, are ready to devour the sheep."[24]

John W. Addison recognized the serious competition in his circuit: "I think of all the cts in the Conf this is one of the greatest for having a few of all kinds of people in it, from Methodists down to Papists, not forgetting Campbellites, and almost every kind of ite and ism in the Creation, and they are as hidebound as the Devil himself."[25]

Peter Cartwright wrote of the disastrous effects of the influence of Campbellism on the ministry of his church. He gave as an example a Methodist minister "fishing in the muddy waters of Campbellism," explaining that he had lost his mental balance. He worried for a considerable time and was carried into "a whirlpool of doubt and disbelief . . . became more and more flighty in his mind till at last in a paroxysm of insanity he shot himself . . . And proves that it is a hard thing to fight against God."[26]

The aloof Episcopalians

The Episcopalians, generally speaking, held aloof of denominational arguments and obvious rivalry. Whereas the Methodists, Baptists, Campbellites, et al., were, in the old tradition, the churches of the common folk, the Episcopalians were regarded as the aristocrats, or the "social" church. Perhaps the following story, as much as any other, will serve to sum up the attitude of this church, as it was held in the popular mind.

At an Episcopal service a parishioner rose and asked: "Pastor, is it possible for a man to achieve salvation outside the fold of the Episcopal Church?"

The pastor stood in deep meditation for a long minute, as if struggling with his soul, the account relates, and then replied: "It is conceivable that there *might* be such a possibility —but no gentleman would avail himself of it."[27]

Owen P. White, a native Texan, and something of a professional scoffer, commented on the Episcopalians in *Lead and Likker:* "Episcopalians, when sober, are not very comical. Moreover, they are far too intelligent to cut much ice in Texas."[28]

The continuous bickering and practice of taking pot shots at rival sects raised the question among impartial observers that doubtless weaknesses existed in all the denominations.

One idealist who would weed out all the weaknesses and hold only the strengths of the various churches made this suggestion for a composite denomination: "If we could get religion like a Baptist, experience it like a Methodist, be positive about it like a Disciple, be proud of it like an Episcopalian, pay for it like a Presbyterian, propagate it like an Adventist, and enjoy it like a Negro—that would be the ideal religion."[29]

The bickering among the denominations doubtless had some ill effects on the over-all promotion of the Christian faith on the frontier. But, on the other hand, the energetic rivalry may have stimulated the devout to greater efforts with the total effect more beneficial than hurtful to the religious movement.

Actually the churches appeared to thrive on controversy. The editor of a Texas Baptist newspaper summed it up pointedly in this fashion: "You know how it is when you hear a horrible squawking from the alley at night and expect to find it littered with dead cats in the morning? But what happens instead is more cats."[30]

Probably no one was ever convinced by the arguments, but the contenders found the discussions "delightfully infuriating."

The rabidness of the frontier in time died down, and though rivalry continued to exist in a fashion, it became good-natured, and church people took to telling jokes about themselves rather than slurring the opposition. Thus the frontier settled down to "civilized disagreement," and gradually "religion civilized first itself and then the frontier."

X

PRAYERS OF THE FRONTIER

Religion on the frontier was a participating affair. Ritual was reduced to the minimum. The individual stood supreme before God. This was the day before sports, entertainment, and religion (as in modern times) became increasingly a spectator activity. On the frontier paid choirs, even paid song leaders, were unheard of. Individuals of the congregation were expected to sound off their praises for the Lord in song, make confessions of their transgressions publicly, and testify for the Lord of what He had done for them, that He might have proper credit and recognition in the eyes of the people, and those weaker in the faith might be encouraged through revealed example.

In the ritual of prayer individualism and the temper of the times showed through most realistically. For the preachers urged everyone to pray, theologian and layman, saint and sinner—privately and publicly.

On the untamed frontier the need of aid from a power beyond that of the backwoods appeared real and constant, even to those of the "little faith" of the proverbial mustard seed.

Because the people truly believed that God was real, and that His spirit abided in this part of the raw earth they were fashioning according to their beliefs, they approached Him as a deity of the backwoods who required little formality or polished manners on the part of His simple children.

Most prayers were too direct and urgent and unsophisticated for concern with rhetoric. Also, the supplicants did not believe in "going through channels." An old Indian fighter said he did not think an intermediary was necessary to get in touch with the Lord; that "when a feller's in a jam, the Lord can hear him if he'll holler."

The people trusted God to have not only understanding of them in their shortcomings, but to have, in some instances, a sense of humor as well. They obviously believed that He heard His earthlings according to their circumstances, whether playful, or scared, or inarticulately confused. One observer expressed the opinion that God hears His children in the light of the wits He gave them.

The frontiersmen apparently held the practical belief that the Deity would understand their problems without explanation or apology, that when one had done the best he knew how . . . well, that was all that could be expected—as in the case of the Texas ranger who got lost in the thicket of a river bottom, and was extremely nervous in the dark, with the possibility of Indians lurking in the shadows. He decided to pray. But the only prayer he could think of was "Now I lay me down to sleep . . ." When he got that far, he stopped with the thought that that was not proper because for him to go to sleep then was the last thing he should do. But after thinking about prayer a while longer, and feeling the increasing need of help beyond his considered means, he decided to go ahead with the one prayer he knew.

He later related that the prayer made him feel better, "though that particular one didn't seem quite right" to him.

Three Oklahoma cowboys, after burying two comrades killed by the Indians felt the need of some sort of ritual. But the problem puzzled and embarrassed them. One of them wrote of the occasion years later. ". . . Someone said that a prayer should be offered. All three of us were uneducated cowboys who had had no chance to attend church services or Sunday school, so none of us knew what to say or do under the circumstances. Both of the other two declined to do what all of us thought should be done, so both said to me, 'Charley, you will have to say something.'

"Now we all believed, as all men who are reared out in the open must and always will believe, that there is a God, who rules and overrules the affairs of men. We had watched the sun, moon, and stars in their courses; we had night herded by the North Star, for years, using it as a time-piece . . . every wind that swept the plains and every note sung by the birds bore witness to the existence of a great, unseen, Divine Power. So knowing the existence of such a Supreme Being, I took off my hat and raised my face to the skies as I said, 'God, take care of these poor boys.' "[1]

They had done their best. Doubtless the cowboys were correct in assuming that the omnipotent Master of the Range expected nothing more elaborate from them.

Often the backwoods folk, not versed in religious etiquette, were embarrassed in the presence of a minister in their home. Circuit rider Horace Bishop told of his visit in a frontier home: "I suggested that we pray before retiring, and the husband said, 'Well, pitch in.' "

At the table, instead of requesting the visiting minister to "ask a blessing," a man once said, "Parson, it's up to you."[2]

The Reverend C. B. Clark, who preached in the mining camps (he preached Calamity Jane's funeral), was called on to give the invocation at a state political convention. The chairman announced: "The Reverend Clark will now entertain us with a devotional prayer."

Circuit rider James H. Addison was disconcerted at what he regarded as a notable lack of piousness on the part of a housewife in whose home he visited. She presented him with the Bible and invited him to "hold prayers." When the prayer started she quietly took up her knitting. When he called her to task about this she insisted upon knitting while he prayed. Many considered idle hands, as well as idle minds, instruments of the devil in those days. Seemingly, it was her custom to pray while knitting, and she saw no reason why it should detract from the effectiveness of the preacher's prayer.[3]

On the unpredictable frontier, urgency of business often took precedence over prayer, though already started. A visiting preacher was saying grace—a lengthy one—during which the host looked out the window and exclaimed: "Cut it short, Parson. The cows are in the garden playing hell with the cabbage."

Among the clergy, practical aspects of prayer varied, in some instances obviously colored by denominational prejudice. In this land where it was generally considered important to get sleep when the opportunity afforded, J. B. Cranfill, a medical doctor as well as a Baptist preacher, took a firm stand against losing unnecessary sleep to pray. He said: "The 6 o'clock prayer meetings are as senseless as they are unnecessary. (In a large measure they are hypocritical. They are advertised and promoted for the purpose of showing forth a degree of piety.) A man can pray just as well after he has arisen from a sound sleep in the regular way and had his breakfast. There is no virtue in jumping out of bed at 5:30, rubbing one's eyes, hastily pulling on one's clothes, and hurrying to some church house to meet a lot of misguided fanatics who think that by disturbing their neighbors, cutting off their natural sleep . . . they can thereby promote righteousness."[4]

Telling God about the need for rain

People lived close to the elements on the frontier. Thus, their prayers were much about the elements, particularly rain. For, before the day of irrigation systems and cloud-seeding for rain making, the people could do no more than plant and trust in a benevolent Providence for a harvest.

The colorful Judge Robert M. Williamson of Texas, better known as "Three-Legged Willie," was noted for his extraordinary prayers. He was often called on to pray at meetings assembled to pray for rain. The following is regarded as typical:

"O Lord, Thou divine Father, the supreme ruler of the Universe, who holdest the thunder and lightning in thy hands, and from the clouds givest rain to make crops for thy children, look down with pity upon thy children who now face ruin for the lack of rain upon their crops; and O Lord, send us a bounteous rain that cause the crops to fruit in all their glory and the earth to turn again to that beauteous green that comes with abundant showers. Lord, send us a bounteous one that will make corn ears shake hands across the row and not one of these little rizzly-drizzly rains that will make nubbins that all hell can't shuck."[5]

Formal "seminary" prayers were not always clear and to the point to some of the old-timers. An old deacon, at a prayer meeting assembled in the hope of gaining relief from an extended drought, was called upon to lead a prayer following a young seminary preacher who had just prayed for "copious showers." The deacon began his supplication by confessing to the Lord that he was not sure what "copious showers" meant, but it didn't sound adequate for his scorched crop. "What we need," he pleaded, "is a pine knot floater and a nubbin stretcher."

Most supplicants pleaded for relief in the way and manner they felt the need. A Hard-Shell Baptist preacher offered this prayer: "Almighty God, thou knowest the wants of us, and we need not be telling you. We have come to this ground to show Thee our penitence and how badly whipped we feel and how willing we are to thank Thee for past blessings and prepare ourselves to thank Thee for the blessings Thou art going to give us in the future. Now, Almighty God, Thou knowest how we are suffering down here, and we want you to come to our relief. We want you to come with no little sprinkle or Pentecostal shower, but, Oh God in Heaven, send us an old-time, old-fashioned gully washer and root-soaker, and be quick about it. Amen."[6]

Deluges, following some dry-weather prayer meetings, prompted some supplicants to caution. They feared they might overstate their needs and thus give the Lord an exaggerated impression of their urgency. One man at a weekly meeting rose and prayed with calculated restraint: "Oh Lord, we need rain bad, send us rain. We don't want a rippin', rarin', tearin', rain that'll harrer up the face of Nature, but a drizzlin', drozzlin', sozzlin' rain, one that'll last all night and putty much all day, Oh Lord."

A rancher, after apparently feeling that he might have pressed the Lord too hard for rain, thought to be more tactful, and at the close of his prayer paused and added as an afterthought: "But after all our petitions, O God, we would not presume to dictate, but we would advise."

Downpours following prayer for rain sometimes brought the supplicants to their knees again to let the Lord know they had had enough. One drought sufferer, suddenly turned flood victim, pleaded: "Lord, Lord, stay thy hand! Enough! Art Thou goin' to drown us out like woodchucks?"

Withering crops brought discouragement, but some farmers considered themselves such apt students of the elements that when the wind turned in the wrong direction their faith was blown away. An old rancher, whose knowledge of his area was greater than his faith, rose in a meeting after several hours of prayer and said: "Brethren, there ain't a bit of use praying for rain as long as the wind is in the west."

Help in battle

Some of the most pressing prayers were voiced in the face of the enemy. The conquerors of the West, arrayed for battle, often prayed for victory, and then set out to help the Lord work a miracle.

The following prayer is attributed to one-time Texas Ranger Captain Jack Hays when his regiment was trapped during the Battle of Palo Alto, a major battle of the Mexican War: "O Lord, we are about to join battle with vastly superior numbers of the enemy, and, Heavenly Father, we would mighty like for you to be on our side and help us. But if You can't do it, for Christ's sake don't go over to the Mexicans, but just lie low and keep in the dark, and You will see one of the dangest fights you've ever seen."

Instead of saying "Amen," Hays roared "Charge!"

Whether or not the exact wording of the prayer has been preserved, it is a historical fact that the Texans fought themselves out of the trap against great odds.

In emergencies of battle expediency often took precedence over tradition. One Indian fighter expressed the belief that prayer called for co-operative action—you ask the Lord for something and then help Him bring it to pass. Having just fought himself out of a tight place after being surrounded by the Indians, he was asked if he had prayed.

He said, "Yes."

Asked if he had closed his eyes to pray, he promptly answered, "No." He explained that if he had closed his eyes the Indians would have gotten him for sure. "I had to keep fightin'. I believe in cooperating with the Lord," he said. "I kinda doubt if the Lord could have gotten me out of that scrape all by Himself."

Many frontiersmen had no hesitancy in calling on the Lord for his co-operation in violent endeavors. During the notorious East Texas feud, known as the War of the Regulators and Moderators, a preacher, tired and disgusted with the killings on both sides, delivered this prayer: "Now, Lord, if any Regulator or Moderator makes any effort to revive their disturbances, curse him with the loss of eyes, destroy his limbs that he may never be able to walk, curse him when he sits down to eat, curse his fields; and if this will not stop his hellish career, kill him and send him down to his own place."

Some immigrants to the western country expressed their worst fright at the first introduction to it, and felt in this moment their greatest need for divine protection against its evils. They seemingly also felt it a duty to keep the Deity alerted as to the conditions of the wild country through which they traveled. A band of immigrants held up their westward journey just outside Dodge City for prayer for protection, during which the minister-leader pleaded: ". . . On our long journey Thy Divine Providence has thus far kept us safe. We have survived cloudbursts, hailstorms, floods, and strong gales, thirst and parching heat—as well as raids of horsethieves and attacks by hostile Indians.

"But now, Oh, Lord, we face our greatest danger. Dodge City lies just ahead, and we must pass through it. Help us and save us, we beseech Thee. Amen."

The leader rose and requested a military escort through Dodge the next day.

The military commander turned down the request. Obviously he, from his on-the-spot observations, did not see the dangers that the immigrants seemingly felt God should see.[7]

Immigrants found enemies in many forms. Some were disturbed over the politics they found in the new country and its influence upon the church. Politics often colored prayer.

A "full-fledged New England Yankee" delivered a sermon south of the Mason-Dixon Line in which he lauded Abraham Lincoln "as a divine creature." At the close of the service a local minister, of the southern persuasion, was called on to pray, during which he said: "Oh Lord, may we follow Abraham Lincoln just as far as he followed the Lord Jesus, and no farther!"[8]

"Don't tell God I'm drunk"

Liquor, directly and indirectly, inspired a great deal of praying.

An old deacon who had a decided weakness for the bottle

got on a terrible bender one night, and thought he was dying. He called his wife, who was a devout woman, and asked her to pray for him. She fell to her knees and prayed: "Oh Lord, have mercy on my poor drunken husband."

The deacon heard her from the next room, and called to her: "No, no, Margaret! Don't tell Him I'm drunk; tell Him I'm sick!"

Ministers, on some occasions, seemed to do a little kidding with the Lord to prod some of the brethren away from the bottle. One pastor offered this prayer for a wayward Nevada miner: "Oh Lord, we pray Thee to remember Brother Brown. Make the rock of his tunnel as soft as his head, and the water in his ditch as abundant as the whiskey he daily drinks. Amen."[9]

A preacher was called into the home of a scoffing, drinking father to pray for the younger son, who had been bitten by a rattlesnake. The stricken boy announced that he had repented. Whereupon the preacher knelt by the side of the bed in the presence of the family, prayed for the bitten boy, and ended his supplication thus: "And we pray Thee, O Lord, to send also a rattlesnake to bite his brother Tom that he may likewise repent of his wickedness and be saved from hell. And we supplicate Thee, O Lord, most earnestly to send another and a larger rattlesnake to bite his father, who has led these fine young men into a life of wickedness, that he may likewise repent of his crimes and turn to Thee before it is too late."[10]

Because of the private nature of much prayer, it is likely a lot more of it is done than is generally supposed. Bad frontiersmen, as well as good, prayed. It is understandable that the bad ones may have felt the greater need for divine aid and direction. Possibly the most noted drinking-hellraising-praying badman on the frontier was Clay Allison.

Some of his neighbors, who observed his antics, and held decided opinions about "Demon Rum," explained that when the spirit of alcohol entered Clay Allison the spirit of the devil entered close behind, that through the transfiguring power of alcohol a reasonably fair Mr. Hyde became a Dr. Jekyll on the rampage.

Many like Allison roamed the wild frontier, and they perhaps sincerely called for divine aid to bring them stability in an unstable (to them) world.

Sometimes Allison was called on to lead in prayer at meetings. But sometimes he turned evangelist and organized his own meetings. One morning in the 1880s he walked into the Lone Wolf Saloon in Pecos, laid two pistols on the end of the bar, and told Red Dick, the bartender, that he intended to turn the saloon into a church for a couple of hours. And he did. He stepped out into the street and rounded up all passers-by and herded them into the saloon—cowboys, merchants, freighters, gamblers, and thugs.

The opening prayer was reported in this fashion:

"Now fellers, we'll pray. Everybody down!"

Only a few knelt. Some regarded the affair as a sacrilege, and others resented dictation. But a slight sweep of Allison's six-shooter brought every man of them to his knees, with heads bowed over faro layouts and monte tables.

"O Lord!" began Allison, "this yere's a mighty bad neck o' woods, an' I reckon You know it. Fellers don' think enough o' their souls to build a church, an' when a pa'son comes here they don' treat him half white. O Lord! make these fellers see that when they gits caught in the final round-up an' drove over the last divide, they don' stan' no sort o' show to git to stay on the heavenly ranch 'n less they believes an' builds a house to pray an' preach in. Right here I subscribes a hundred dollars to build a church, an' if airy one o' these fellers don' ante up accordin' to his means, O Lord, make it Your pers'n'l business to see that he wears the Devil's brand and ear mark an' never gits another drop o' good spring water.

"Of course, I allows You knows I don' sport no wings myself, but I want to do what's right ef You'll sort o' give me a shove the proper way. An' one thing I want You to understan'; Clay Allison's got a fast horse an' is tol'ably handy with his rope, and he's goin' to run these fellers into Your corral even if he has to rope an' drag 'em there. Amen. Everybody git up!"

While he "prayed in the most reverent tone he could command, and while his attitude was one of simple supplication, Mr. Allison never removed his keen eyes from the congregation."[11]

And who is there to say of this how much was prank and how much worship?

Moderation was not a virtue

It was characteristic of the frontiersmen to go all out whether for good or evil. Moderation was not considered a virtue, even in prayer. Whether a bullying Clay Allison or an evangelistic devotee like R. C. Burleson, the energy of the new country coming alive surged in them.

Burleson prayed: "O God, give me Texas for Christ, or I die . . . Even so, Lord Jesus, come quickly."

When the pioneers prayed for power they frequently asked for the full measure of it. The preachers pleaded for strength to raise themselves and their sheep up to "march on higher ground," and they were direct and to the point about their requests—no dilly-dallying or beating about the bush with the Lord who was seeing this vast untamed hinterland through the valley.

The following prayer, somewhat typical in spirit, is attributed to a Negro pastor: "Oh, Lawd, gib Thy servant dis marnin' de eyes of de eagle an' de wisdom of de owl; connect his soul wid de Gospel in de skies; 'luminate his brow wid de sun of hebben; pizzen his mind wid love for de people; turpentine his 'magination; grease his lips wid possum oil; loosen his tongue wid de sledge hammer of Thy power; 'lectrify his brain wid de lightnin' of Thy word; put 'petual motion in his ahms; fill him plum full of de dynamite of Thy glory; 'noint him all ovah wid de oil of Thy salvation an' set him on fire. Amen."[12]

The frontier folk possessed such a capacity to laugh at themselves they told funny stories about prayer. Where truth ends and fiction begins is sometimes difficult to say. If the stories are not fact they are caricatures, which, in a sense, may reveal more truth than documents. They are believed because they reveal the heights of man's hope, and the mortal flaws in his faith.

All-out faith in immediate answer to prayer is illustrated in a story of an old maid who, feeling that her opportunities for matrimony were fast coming to an end, went out into the woods, greatly distressed, to meditate upon the matter. She finally concluded that since there was no earthly hope in sight she would call upon the Lord for help. She knelt down and prayed fervently: "Oh Lord, hear my prayers. This day send me a man. Send me a man, Oh Lord, that I may not be lonesome."

At that moment an owl in a nearby tree sounded out: "Who! Who! Who!"

The old maid jumped to her feet and shouted with joy: "Anybody, Lord. Just anybody!"[13]

A certain sister weary of the woes of this world went out to a place near a high bank, knelt and requested of the Lord that if it was His will, she might be taken from this world of sin and sorrow to a better one where she might rest. While thus praying, a slight earth shock occurred and some of the bank fell off and struck her on the back. She jumped up, brushed the dirt off, and exclaimed: "Well! I do declare. What's this world a-comin' to? Nowadays everything a body says is taken in yearnest."[14]

A woman hearing a sermon on faith and its power to move mountains, if one had a sufficient amount of it, prayed that night that a hill which rose in front of her cabin and obstructed her view might be moved.

Next morning she hurried to the front door to view the results of her faith.

Seeing the hill still in place, she turned away in disgust, and said: "Just as I expected."[15]

The great deterrent to faith was impatience. An old Louisiana deacon had two grown sons who got into a terrible fight with each other. The father did everything he could to make peace between them, but his effort brought no results. In desperation he hurried to his pastor and implored him to act as peacemaker: "Brother Brown, I want you to talk to my boys, and see if you can stop them from fighting. I'm afraid they are going to kill each other."

"Have you prayed about the matter?" the preacher asked.

"Yes. I have," the deacon answered. "But I want something done now. Prayer is powerful sure, but it's so slow."

In spite of disappointments and human frailties, faith remained strong and simple on the frontier. It sustained the builders of the new land when their enemies were legion beyond their knowing and lurked in the darkness where only the Supreme Protector knew; when subsistence was given or taken with defeating suddenness by the elements and the helplessness of mortals to control them was manifested daily.

The documented account of Sam W. Moreland will illustrate this trust in prayer which sustained the faithful when they could not reckon with the morrow alone.

There were many Sam Morelands on the raw, Indian-infested hinterlands when the mettle of this country was being tempered.

Moreland was attending a camp meeting about the year 1884 when a band of raiding Indians swept across his range. One of the men who had trailed the marauders came to the meeting and reported the raid: "They got all your horses, Brother Moreland," the messenger announced.

Moreland was sitting in his tent when he heard the news. He put his elbows on his knees and his face in his hands and sat thus for a moment, then he rose up and said: "I can't believe they got my big bunch of horses."

"Why?" the messenger inquired.

Moreland replied: "When my wagons were loaded and all started to the camp ground, I went back into my house and on my knees I told God I was going down to worship and asked Him to take care of all my affairs; I believe He has done it."

He ordered a servant to saddle his horse, and he rode away toward home.

Later in the day he returned and took his seat among the congregation. All knew why Brother Moreland had been absent, and the minister in the pulpit, sensing the concern of the people, halted his sermon momentarily for Brother Moreland to report.

"Not a horse gone," he said.

And the sermon went on, as if that was exactly what everybody expected to hear.

XI

SCOFFERS AND TROUBLEMAKERS

A common sport of disbelievers and pranksters was the effort to break up church services and heckle preachers. Sometimes these efforts created mere nuisances or temporary distractions. But in some instances they forced church leaders to meet violence with violence, even to the use of guns.

On the frontier, where entertainment was strictly home-made, church services offered excellent and convenient opportunities for scoffers to have fun. Preachers often had to take due precautions.

In one community a group of rowdy boys, having observed the unrestrained emotions of penitents, impassioned by religious excitement and subject to unreserved demonstrations, decided to go to church and take advantage of this condition and hug the girls.

It was planned that the leader would come to the bench as a penitent for prayer. His gang would follow. They planned to "all get religion" at the same time, and then "go around hugging all the girls."

This seemed to the boys a superb scheme to have some exciting fun with the girls that might result in just about anything, including breaking up the meeting or starting a riot.

Preachers made it their business to stay alert to such designs. The evangelist, in this instance, got wind of the plot, and learned the identity of the leader. When the leader came and knelt, the evangelist, a large strong man, came and knelt over him immediately, exhorting him loudly to repentance and prayer, beating out a rhythm on the "penitent's" back that fairly knocked the breath out of him.

By the time the preacher let him up he had all thoughts of amour beaten out of him. Once out from under the preacher's heavy hand, he headed straight for the church door without so much as a look toward the girls.[1]

Some scoffers would do almost anything to be ornery, or to get a laugh. A group of rowdies decided it was much more fun to break up a song service than to sing, brought a strong-lunged hen to a revival meeting, stationed themselves under an open window of the church, and when the congregation sang, the gang's leader would make the hen squawk. Not only were the discordant notes of the agitated hen a distraction from those of the hymn, but some members of the congregation, more easily attracted by earthly doings than those of the spirit, could not restrain laughter at the ludicrous contrasts of sounds and efforts.

Peter Cartwright wrote of a routine designed by backwoods scoffers to drown out preachers and break up church services: "They began at a distance to bark like dogs, and howl like wolves; they drew nearer and nearer and crowed like chickens." But they did not show themselves.

These fun-makers had good reason to do their howling in the distance, outside the church, when Cartwright was preaching. For nothing riled Peter Cartwright into holy indignation like scoffers trying to interfere with the Lord's work, particularly if he was representing the Lord at that time. And his reputation being well known for being just as ingenious, determined, and violent as the worst of them in determining that the Lord got a fair shake where he was conducting services, most scoffers created their disturbances at a discreet distance. Expediency came before dignity and formality with Cartwright. He fought the devil's fire with his own brand of it. When Scripture and persuasion did not prove adequate, he resorted to fist and club, and was just as adept—and often more effective—with the latter. He gave more than one skull a sound cracking to bring order where he was preaching.

On one occasion he was praying with two sisters at the altar while their disbelieving mother looked on disapprovingly nearby. When she thought Cartwright was too busy with his praying and was not watching she would kick the daughters in their sides in the attempt to drive them up from their knees.

If Cartwright had not written a firsthand account we might be inclined to doubt the indelicate measure he resorted to "to defeat the scheme of the devil again." "I took hold of her [the mother's] foot [the kicking foot, we presume] and gave her a strong push backwards."

It must have been a tremendous, upsetting push by the strong-armed Cartwright that sent the woman sprawling, bottom side up several rows back into the congregation. For as he told it: ". . . Over she tumbled among the benches. Being a large, corpulent woman, she had some considerable tussle to right herself again." Having been tossed into her embarrassed position by the evangelist himself, chivalry apparently was momentarily stunned into inaction; and the distressed scoffer was forced to right herself from the spectacle she had made as best she could.

Cartwright assumed the attitude that with the Lord on your side you couldn't lose, and he led others to his views. The heavier the devil's shackles appeared to bind sinners, the more determined he was to unshackle them. And with humanity "hair-hung and breeze-shaken over hell" a preacher could not afford to loiter for a minute. He reported that he "later prayed with this [same] woman and brought her to conversion that same day."[2]

The preacher who gained respect on the frontier usually

had to demand it—and he could not be wishy-washy about it.

Preachers not only had to contend with scoffing unbelievers, they sometimes found good-intentioned church members natural-born nuisances. A sprinkling of them are found in church as almost anywhere else, and can be a strain on a pastor's patience and self-control. Cartwright once had one that was almost more than he could bear. And being a forthright man, he did not pussyfoot, even with the delicate sex. His "cross" was an old lady, as noisy as she was pious, who often annoyed him and disturbed his meetings by "going off on a high key." In a class meeting one day when her soul was filled with ecstatic emotions, she rapturously cried out, "If I had one more feather in my wing of faith, I would fly away and be with my Savior!"

Cartwright, without hesitation, shouted: "Stick in the other feather, Lord, and let her go!"[3]

Sometimes a person broke up a service without intending to do it. J. T. Griswold told of holding a meeting in a crowded schoolroom one hot August night. A giant of a fellow came in late and took the only vacant seat, about two feet in front of the little table the preacher used. The table was large enough to hold only a small tin bucket of water and a dipper, the preacher's Bible, and a kerosene lamp.

Griswold reported sympathetically that the man had been running a hay press all day, and was tired, and that soon he stretched his long legs under the middle of the table and went sound asleep. But when the tired man began to snore, almost in the preacher's face, that was too much. At least, the preacher decided to make some capital of the situation to illustrate the sermon he was preaching on the subject of "lukewarmness." "There are people in this church as sound asleep as this man right here," he shouted, leaning over and putting his finger near the man's open mouth.

The man awoke with a terrible start, kicking the table over, sending water splashing in all directions, on the preacher and the congregation. The dipper hit the wall, "making enough noise for a score of such vessels." Bedlam broke out. Children screamed, the young people laughed, the dogs started barking hysterically, which so alarmed the horses that a number broke their tethers and ran away. Possible holocaust was avoided by the preacher, who with supreme agility and presence of mind, managed to catch the lamp.[4]

That ended the service.

The preacher used his stick

Preachers often had to be policemen, in the true sense of the term, and demand respect with more realistic substance than Scripture and personal dignity.

Z. N. "Wildcat" Morrell's most conspicuous accouterment was a heavy walking stick, which he used effectively on occasion to bring a reverent atmosphere to church services. One evening some rowdies, including a large Negro man, bent on some high fun at mockery came to one of Morrell's meetings. When the service got under way the Negro man proceeded to stick his head inside the church through an open window and shout "Glory to God!" His cohorts responded with loud "Amens!"

After a few outbursts, when the Reverend Morrell was not leading the service, he eased from the pulpit and along the wall where the head was coming into the church. And the next time it came in, it got out only "Glory t'," when the preacher's hickory stick came down on it with such force that the glory of mockery forever left the scoffer. And his pals were so busy ministering to his immediate needs they had neither the time nor stomach for further scoffing that evening.

Some preachers made effective use of guns in and out of church. "Fightin'" Jack Potter arrived at Sabinal Canyon, Texas, to preach one Saturday night at the end of a sixty-mile ride through dangerous country, and was told by the presiding elder that because of a large, mostly drunken crowd that had gathered for horse racing that day, the meeting should be called off. He insisted that the noisy, drunken gang would break up church.

"Fightin'" Jack looked at the elder for a long moment, then said: "You ever heard of anybody breaking up one of my meetings?"

"But you haven't seen this gang. They're keyed up for trouble. There could be bloodshed if anybody tried to interfere with their devilment."

Potter told the elder to announce services, that he had traveled sixty miles to preach, and he would preach as scheduled.

That night a sizable crowd assembled, including the boisterous horse-racing gang. Potter waited until the congregation was well assembled. Then he made his entrance. He walked gravely down the aisle with his revolver belt hanging conspicuously on his left arm, and his famous Winchester carried in his right hand. A hush fell over the buzzing assembly. Reaching the stand he hung his gun belt on a nail on the wall at the back of the pulpit in clear view of the audience, leaned his Winchester against a chair in easy reach, and proceeded calmly without a word of introduction or threat, to read Scripture, sing, pray, and preach. A man who attended the service reported that he had never seen a quieter, better behaved audience.[5]

Preaching to desperados

Preaching could be downright dangerous when conspicuous, sensitive sinners took what the preacher said about sin as personal. Most people who went to church were prepared to take whatever the preacher dished out about wicked ways. And unless he called names one could usually think of someone else he was talking about when he enumerated certain vices. But some outstanding sinners were touchy about what was said, even to speaking disparagingly about the particular class of sin they indulged in, and they did not consider that the pulpit afforded liberty to "cast reflections."

Ben Moore, in his biography of the Reverend A. E. Butterfield, tells of a preacher threatened by desperados during a revival in Mills County, Texas. He was told to quit preaching against sin in their community or take the consequences. The preacher, knowing the reputation of the desperados, did not have to do much speculation as to what they meant by the consequences. He did not stop preaching against sin, but he did take the precaution to bring his Winchester to each service and place it within arm's reach.

"With the falling of brimstone on their heads," at a service a few evenings later, one of the badmen jumped to his feet and fired at the evangelist, "cutting a neat swath through his hair just above one ear." Without losing his composure the preacher put a bullet squarely between the would-be assassin's eyes. A second desperado jumped to his feet, as if to draw, but realizing the quick draw and deadly aim of the preacher, as demonstrated on his pal, he apparently considered a hasty retreat the better part of valor. But he hesitated for a moment. The preacher took no chances. He did, however, spare the man's life, but only after securing his own by putting a bullet through the man's shooting arm.[6]

Some scoffers would go to almost any length to pull a caper in church. Evangelist L. M. White told of an odd case during one of his revivals. One night when he called for penitents a big six-foot-tall man came down the aisle wearing two six-shooters, large roweled spurs and carrying a quirt on his wrist, and knelt at the altar with a number of others. White called on his mother to lead the prayer. In the midst of the prayer the big, armed man began to jump and shout, and every time he jumped he managed to bring the rowels of his spurs down upon one of the penitents, and "with his quirt he was stripping everybody."

White later told of the affair, which gives a vivid insight into preacher policing: "I looked up just in time to see the villain bring down his quirt with all his force upon my poor mother's shoulder blades. All the devil that was in me arose at that moment. I grabbed him by the collar, and the next best hold, and stood him on his head out the door. He reached for his gun, but I beat him to the draw, and sticking my Remington into his eyes made him crawl into a wagon . . . Just at that time, with everybody excited, a regular pandemonium reigning, I threw my Remington on the crowd and howled, 'Sit down! We came here to worship God, and we are going to do it if I have to kill somebody.' A good religious song was started . . . The spirit of heavenly peace seemed to hover, and a glorious meeting with many converts was the result."[7]

Often a threat from the preacher sufficed. Once when a heckler bothered James Ferguson (father of Governor Jim Ferguson of Texas), he stopped his sermon and said: "I can fight as well as preach, and if you will wait until I finish this sermon, I'll attend to you next." James Ferguson bore the title of "Fighting," and no one ever accused him of bluffing. The heckling stopped.

As a rule, the preacher was the chief police force at church. He did not get the spontaneous aid from the brethren that he frequently needed. But sometimes it came as unsolicited as it was welcomed. There could not have been any more sudden and complete relief from a heckler than that rendered on one occasion by James Bowie, who designed and made the bowie knife famous. He had come to church to hear a sermon, but the preacher was being heckled so loudly and persistently he was having great difficulty making himself heard by the congregation. Finally Bowie rose and announced that if there was any further misconduct he would take care of it by cutting off the wind of the offender. "I'm Jim Bowie," he concluded.

When Jim Bowie talked of cutting, men either backed up or went for their knives. In this instance the man shut up, and the preacher had a model congregation.[8]

Bringing "Prairie Dog" to church

Some scoffers were merely nuisances with a prankish turn of mind. But the frontier brand of pranks was often a rough variety. The baptistery in which Sam Houston was to be baptized was filled with treetops the night before by mischievous boys. The distinguished statesman and the congregation had to travel to a distant creek for the ceremony.

Sometimes the rugged settlers looked upon the pious clergymen as made of too flimsy stuff for their wild country, and devised their own examinations to test their mettle. Brit Bailey, noted Texas cattle baron and individualist, was home one evening relaxing over his cups when a Methodist minister rode up to his house and asked for lodging. Bailey accepted him on the condition that he would abide by "the rules of the house." The minister agreed.

After supper Bailey reminded the preacher of his promise, took a rifle from the rack, leveled it on him, directed him to undress, get upon a table, and dance a jig. The preacher had no other recourse. So while a Negro servant scraped out a jig tune on a fiddle, the preacher did the best he could at dancing until Bailey called a halt.

The preacher got down, redressed, and the men sat by the fire continuing their talk—until the preacher caught his host off guard, grabbed the rifle, and put him through the identical routine.

Bailey could take a joke as well as play one. He admired the preacher's courage, and the two became fast friends.

It is difficult to understand this rugged sense of humor and horseplay with a minister without knowing something about Brit Bailey. He was such an individualist that he was, by his own demand, buried standing up. Even after death, he said, he would look up to no man.[9]

Prairie Dog Dave of Dodge City was not exactly a scoffer; he just got good and tired of preachers' pestering him to come to church when he didn't want to. Finally one ambitious rov-ing evangelist, knowing of Prairie Dog Dave's stubborn repu-tation, asked a committee to go out and bring him in.

The committee brought Prairie Dog into Rowdy Kate's dance hall, where boards had been strung over beer barrels for seats and a pulpit arranged at one end of the hall. He sat down sullenly on a faro table in the rear, while the minister delivered a sermon on the subject of being ready to die.

Finally he could endure no more. He rose up, and in a strong voice addressed the preacher: "Mister, do you mean to say you're livin' thet away, so good thet you're ready to cash in any old time?"

"Yes, sir, I am," the evangelist answered.

"Then you better die right now, when you're settin' purty," Prairie Dog shouted, as he pulled two six-shooters and started picking up splinters at the preacher's feet. The preacher let out a yell and dived behind a row of kegs.

Prairie Dog blew the smoke out of his guns and said: "Boys, you see he's no more ready to die than I am."

So far as the records reveal, future evangelists were content to let Prairie Dog Dave remain away from church.[10]

Some scoffers considered it great fun to see a clergyman forced into undignified acts or positions. Father Vital Quinon, who built a number of churches in Texas, went into a public hall one day to collect funds for a new church. A couple of spreeing bullies sighted the priest, and decided it would be hilarious to have him do one of his church acts in the saloon. So they approached him and told him they wanted to hear him pray. He protested that it was neither the place nor the hour for formal prayer. But with two guns in the hands of reckless drinkers nudging his sides he dropped to his knees and prayed audibly while the bullies made loud comments, laughed gleefully, and pointed out the spectacle to the other customers.

Shortly afterward, while traveling on a missionary trip, Fa-ther Quinon encountered one of his abusers on the road. Having a gun on him, he covered the man, and demanded that he dismount from his horse, kneel and pray. The man gave as an excuse that he did not know how to pray.

The priest looked over his gun sights at the man, and in no uncertain tones, said: "Son, I'll teach you how to pray." And there by the roadside, with a gun barrel in the face of the kneeling man, he made him learn "Our Father."[11]

Scripture alone did not bring respect for God and church to the frontier, but in the hands of determined, fearless men it came—a little slowly, but surely.

XII

THE HARD LOT OF SADDLEBAG PREACHERS

Frontier ministers endured a greater variety of hardships than any other class of its people. It has been aptly said that the saddlebag preachers often outworked the farmer, outrode the hunter, and outdistanced the fur trader. They not only possessed the drive that comes of spiritual dedication, they were men of vigor, strength, and self-reliance—they had to be to survive. They apparently took the apt phrase of William Penn literally: "No Cross, No Crown."

The historian Sweet said of early Baptist preachers (it was much the same for others): They "lived and worked exactly as did their flocks; their dwellings were little cabins with dirt floors, and instead of bedsteads, skin-covered polebunks: they cleared the ground, split rails, planted corn, and raised hogs on equal terms with their parishioners."[1]

On the sparsely settled frontier the preachers spent much of their time traveling. Before the end of the eighteenth century John Clark made preaching tours south of St. Louis that often covered twelve hundred miles, much of it by foot and canoe.

Peter Cartwright wrote of his travels: "We crossed creeks

and large rivers without bridges or ferry-boats, often swam them on horseback, or crossed on trees that had fallen over the streams, drove our horses over and often waded out waist deep; and if by chance we got a dugout, or canoe, to cross in ourselves and swim our horses by, it was quite a treat."[2]

Methodist Horace Bishop told of making the rounds of his circuit: "I preached twenty-eight times a month. I never took breakfast and dinner at the same place except on Friday, which was laundry day in the country . . . My wardrobe was one end of my saddlebags; my bookcase the other end . . . My 'study' was the shade of any tree on the way to my appointments, where there was grass for my horse . . . I slept wherever it was convenient, on a sheepskin or my Mexican blanket, occasionally on a dirt or a puncheon floor."[3]

One circuit rider estimated that the bare earth was their bed three fourths of the time winter or summer, with "a saddle for their pillow and the sky for their coverlet."

The English writer, Frederick Marryat, related that it was a "well-known fact that there is a species of bronchitis or affection of the lungs peculiar to the ministers of the United States, arising from their labours in their profession."[4]

But rather than hardships of travels, the ministers spoke mainly of success. Daniel Buckner summed up his travels in the service: "The church gave me a horse and I rode down many a wild goat, and gathered in many a wandering sheep."[5]

Travelers rarely found comfortable accommodations. Housing space on the frontier was always at a premium, limited, as a rule, to bare family necessities. Bishop Asbury wrote of the generous-minded but poor pioneers: "But kindness will not make a crowded log cabin, twelve feet by ten, agreeable: Without are cold and rain; and within, six adults and as many children, one of which is all motion; the dogs too sometimes must be admitted . . . I found that among my other trials, I had taken the itch."[6] Considering the many dirty beds the bishop had slept in, he marveled that he had not caught it twenty times more.

Walter Smith South made an entry in his diary concerning a night's lodging: "Was so troubled with bed bugs that I could not sleep—a very common thing in that country when one sleeps in the house, but this we seldom do in the summer time."[7]

Littleton Fowler told of sleeping on a hard bed on the floor with two brothers, and twice during the night awakening to find himself on the floor with no cover over him.

The Indian danger

Indians posed a constant menace to the preachers traveling the outer perimeter. Many by expert marksmanship saved themselves to preach another day. As basic precaution, they often traveled armed to the teeth and made it a practice to lay a pistol and the Bible side by side on the lectern. When necessity demanded, they dismissed services to lead, or accompany, the brethren to fight Indians. A good number of preachers earned the title of "Fighting" because of their survival of battles with Indians.

Peter W. Gravis wrote of his assignment to "outside territory": "As I was light for running and small to shoot at by the Indians, the bishop gave me the outside row."[8]

Preachers did not always come out unscathed. Pleasant Tackett, while riding a mule on a circuit to preach in homes of settlers on the outside fringe, was chased by Indians and hit in the foot with an arrow. He reached down, pulled the arrow out, and used it to "increase the mule's speed."[9] John Strange traveled from blockhouse to blockhouse in Indiana Territory. If he found all the settlers still safe from Indian depredations upon arriving at his destination, he led the singing of a hymn that began "And are we yet alive."

The ministers seemingly took these dangers as routine; and trusting in Providence, a fast mount, alertness, and good marksmanship, they traveled undauntedly through savage-infested vineyards just as they did in more protected ones. A colleague spoke of "Fighting" Ephraim McDonald "armed with double-barrel gun chasing back the Indians and sowing gospel seed all over. . . ."[10]

It should be pointed out that once the Indians had an opportunity to know the preachers firsthand they usually held them in special respect among the whites. Badger Clark told of "Preacher Smith," who "walked into Deadwood Gulch in April 1876, while the placer miners were still whipsawing boards to make sluices," and started holding Sunday services. One day while walking through the woods to a preaching appointment at another camp he was shot, apparently by raiding Indians. "His body was found beside the trail, unmutilated and decently laid out. It would seem that the Indians regretted their hasty shot when Smith's black coat and Bible told them what manner of man he was. They had learned that members of the clergy did not lie to them or try to cheat and debauch them."[11]

They received $40 a year

Many of the basic hardships of the frontier preachers resulted from lack of financial support by the church and lack of time from religious duties to properly support themselves and families. The pioneers in general, and the preachers themselves to a great extent, took the position that it was the ordained lot of preachers to be poor and kept humble. Most frontier people would have gazed with astonishment at a man hat in hand passing through their congregation, begging money for their preacher. If the preacher managed to earn money elsewhere for his support, that was admirable enough, but something entirely different from collecting it in church. One brother called upon to donate to a preacher because he had ridden a long distance answered that he deserved no pay because he had ridden just as far to hear the preacher. A Baptist minister contended that his denomination was so stingy in supporting its preachers that its doctrine might be stated: "The Lord keep thee humble, and we'll keep thee poor."

Bishop Asbury felt that the presence of too many worldly goods would cause a diminution of zeal and spirituality among his preachers. He is said on one occasion to have "prayed to the Lord to keep the preachers poor." One historian observed that this prayer was not necessary.

A Methodist circuit rider's yearly salary prior to 1800 was $64 plus a small traveling allowance. In 1800 the stipend was raised to $80, and in 1816 to $100. This was the amount allowed. Collecting it was something else. Peter Cartwright observed that a single circuit rider seldom received more than $30 to $40 a year, and often much less, and that married ones were "starved into location."

An Arkansas minister, running for the state legislature, discovered that the only thing his opponent could say against him was that he was a preacher. He defended himself with the proposition that maybe he actually was not a preacher, for he replied in this fashion: "I have thought that I was a preacher, but in the ten years that I have been trying it, I have received $8 and 12 watermelons, so the folks do not seem to think that I am a preacher to hurt."[12]

When Horace Bishop was sent as a missionary to Hearne, Texas, he expected no salary, for, as he said, "There was no missionary appropriation, as the Board had nothing to appropriate but prayers." The only thing furnished him was a room to preach in, over a saloon, and the owner refused to close on Sunday during church time or stop his brass band from playing.[13]

Even people who paid the preacher often took odd attitudes about it. A steward contributed as quarterage one hundred pounds of bacon. At the quarterly meeting the brother brought in his bill charging fifteen cents a pound. Objection was made to the price in view of the current market price of ten cents. The steward admitted that he would not expect to get more than ten cents in town for it. When asked why he charged the preacher more, he explained that all he gave to the church was exactly so much treasure laid up in heaven. He considered it important to put his bacon at a high price that it might swell his heavenly account as much as possible.

One preacher was flabbergasted to find a Southerner during the last days of the Civil War taking consolation in the fact that Confederate money had gone down in buying power to virtually nothing. He said it was good for one thing—it would pay the preacher. And that was what he paid him with —at the pre-inflation rate.[14]

Generosity sometimes startled preachers, it was so rare. W. L. Harris, a poor Methodist preacher, was walking in the road one day when he was overtaken by a big, rough-looking man wearing a gun in his belt, who addressed him bluntly: "Are you a Methodist preacher?" Harris hesitated for a moment, not knowing whether the man might be a scoffer bent on trouble. The man continued: "I have been looking for one for several days, and you are the only one that looks anything like one I have seen."

Harris admitted that he was a Methodist preacher.

The man looked relieved, and said: "I saw my old shouting Methodist mother in a dream several nights ago and she told me to give some money to the first Methodist preacher I saw, so here is twenty-five dollars."

Harris hesitated again. He was accustomed to laboring for nothing, but to receive such a large amount from a man he had never seen before, had him nonplused. But as soon as he gained his composure he decided that a preacher, of all people, should not look a gift horse in the mouth, took the money, and both men went happily their ways.[15]

The preachers themselves were, in a great measure, responsible for their low pay. Obviously they did not preach on tithing. Certainly not effectively. Many doubtless took the attitude that the heavier their Cross here, the brighter their Crown hereafter. One historian made the observation that the ministers expected little pay for their services and were seldom disappointed in their expectations.

During the anti-missionary squabble, based mainly on money, a leader said the very method of the missionary preachers to get money was "disgustful to common modesty." He compared them to Judas "who was a lover of money and to the horse leech which sucks blood with great vigor."[16]

Preachers who were "corrupted" into going off to answer calls where the pay was higher were called "Greenback" preachers by their colleagues who remained behind.

Some preachers willing to accept better pay considered it more trouble to collect than it was worth. A preacher, told by one of his parishioners that his congregation was considering raising his salary, replied: "I beg you not to think of such a thing, for it is about as much business to collect my present salary as I wish to attend to; if it should be increased, I should be obliged to devote my whole time to collecting it."[17]

The Praying Band of San Francisco

Lay workers as well as ministers faced discouragements. Perhaps most discouragement to the devout came from seeing their labors go ineffective, or seeing sheep, once thought secure, wander from the fold. One of the most notable last "sinkholes of iniquity" on the frontier was the Barbary Coast in San Francisco. Its wildness began with the gold rush to California in 1849. And many of the West's most colorful characters—both famous and infamous—had a part in its sordid drama.

The case of Happy Jack Harrington and the Praying Band will illustrate the difficulty of replacing vileness with decency because Happy Jack was one of the most picturesque of the hardened devotees to the assorted sins of the area, and the Praying Band was about as dedicated and persistent a band of women as were ever inspired by the missionary spirit to leave home and go slumming.

These pious ladies faced hardships, abuse, and danger—with little to show for their efforts. Some pessimistic observers urged the Praying Band to wait—that only time in its own due course could right the Barbary Coast. But America at this time was growing big and fast, and the frontier was the part where the shoots of growth were springing out, for better or worse. Discouragement was never much of a factor in the expanding frontier, and the most unlikely to be discouraged were the devout—dead-set on bringing this country up in "God's way." It was a routine practice for the Praying Band to surround a drunken man and ask him pointedly: "Have you seen Jesus?" Few answered in the affirmative or showed any inclination to seek Him.

But one day in early 1878 when it seemed that "bringing the light" to this place of horrible darkness was a lost cause, some members of the band found Happy Jack most unhappy, recovering from an attack of delirum tremens. He was immobile under the circumstances, and the band zeroed in on him in mass. By the time his mind had escaped from the fearsome realm of purple crocodiles and pink elephants the ladies had filled it instead with visions of a happier land in the "sweet by-and-by."

He took the pledge, professed religion, and announced that he was changing his ways completely. The Praying Band rejoiced in this accomplishment, regarding it as one of the brightest stars in their crowns; and Harrington set out to adjust his business in accordance with his new life. This meant considerable sacrifice of finance and prestige, for Happy Jack owned the Opera Comique, on Murderer's Corner, a combination saloon and bawdy house, the most obscene and profitable on the Barbary Coast.

Happy Jack sold his dive and established a little restaurant on California Street away from the temptations of the Coast. The Praying Band pointed out Happy Jack's conversion and his now happy state as an object lesson, hopeful that others would follow his example. Instead, his friends held him in contempt. But most discouraging to the band—less than a month after his "conversion" he was found lying drunk in the gutter before his new restaurant, his Bible clasped to his breast.

As if this were not set-back enough to the Praying Band, Happy Jack not only went back into business on the Barbary Coast, he hated the Praying Band so intensely that he engaged an auditorium, Platt's Hall, and announced that he would lecture on "The True Inwardness of the Gospel Temperance Movement, or, The Potato Peeled." He hired a brass band for the occasion.

On the rostrum he complained that he had been financially ruined by the influence of the Praying Band, that in order to get a stake to go into business again he had had to resort to marked cards. He lamented that his beautiful Spanish and French dancers were gone and his best friend, Dutch Louise, had married another man. "I stand before you a frightful example of the destructive effects of temperance."[18]

The crowd cheered. And welcomed Happy Jack back. He spoke their language—the language of the only world they knew or were concerned with.

Hardships for the ladies of the Praying Band increased. Men spat uncomfortably close to them when they passed by. And women of the Coast made obscene remarks in their hearing to show that they did not want them there.

Though Happy Jack Harrington and his followers put up positive, active competition, the Praying Band kept right on praying, and preaching a better way of life, until ultimately a better way of life did replace debauchery on the Barbary Coast. Precisely what amount of the credit can be given to the Praying Band and the ministers, and how much should go to law enforcement, the march of civilization, and natural phenomena, cannot be said. But it is a historical fact that the missionaries, though frequently slowed up, never gave up. And such is basically the story of the taming of the wild frontier.

The unheralded wives of preachers

Preachers' wives shared in the hardships and destitution of their sacrificing husbands. And theirs was an unheralded role. Perhaps no group of women ever labored so tirelessly, and made so little fuss about it, in the effort to aid their husbands to put up the best possible front in public.

The Reverend W. T. Tardy, in *The Man and the Message*,[19] said that not infrequently when the minister's wife does have her day and is "lauded on the rostrum . . . as the queen of the preacher's heart, the joy of his home and the crown of his life and the same old sweetheart as she was in the beginning, [she] is at home a pinched, over-worked little woman of great common sense and marvelous industry who probably has not a suitable dress to accompany her . . . husband to his meeting."

Only at separation of the minister from his family has this writer found record of complaint. A Methodist minister, transferred from Mexia to Fort Worth, Texas, could not raise the money necessary to take his wife and family with him. So he directed her to "visit her folks" in a nearby town until he could get the money to rent a house and pay the freight charges on their furniture. The disappointed and exasperated wife replied: "Pa and ma both prophesied that if I married a Methodist preacher I would come to this."

Three weeks passed before the preacher received any money, and then only twenty-five cents. At the end of four weeks, at a conference, he met a stranger, and told him of his plight of being separated from his family. The stranger did not contribute anything to his salary, or make a gift, but he did lend him fifty dollars, and allowed him four years to pay it back.

The minister wrote of his joy and hurry at the prospect of being reunited with his wife and family: "I jumped into my buggy and did not halt my speed until I reached Fort Worth . . . The next morning I had all my furniture out of the depot." He wired his wife: "Now you can come; the house is ready." ". . . We were both shouting happy when she and the babies sat around the little stove that night."

Then he was off "constantly visiting the circuits and stations." And what was the long-separated wife doing now that she was happily rejoined with her husband? "She was sewing and making enough to pay for the grocery bills. Many a night she sewed until midnight."[20]

And so they lived happily and poorly together ever after.

The humble beginnings of churches

Frontier clergymen never waited for a church in order to start preaching. They held services just about any place where good-intentioned people would collect—in the open, in homes, saloons, gambling halls, and under brush arbors. They did not wait for big things. All they usually had in the beginning was faith—the cornerstone of most frontier churches.

W. J. Joyce related: "I organized a church at one place under a spreading live oak tree with one member, a poor widow . . . My successors kept up the appointments, and now, after forty-six years, a fine congregation worships in a good church built near the tree."[21]

Preachers often improvised a frontier cabin or kitchen into a sanctuary. This often took superb control and concentration. J. R. Brisco was preaching in a small cabin home that served also as a smokehouse. He stood behind a plain pine table, and over him, suspended from the joists hung huge sides of bacon, plump hams, and strings of sausages. When warmed up, in a violent gesticulation, he swung his hand up and struck a side of bacon, bringing it down with a thud at his feet.

Without a break in his remarks, he grasped it on two sides, raised it to the table, spread a large bandanna over it, laid the large family Bible on it, and proceeded as if nothing had happened.[22]

Such poor assembly circumstances sometimes contributed

to poor results. The devout often claimed that the devil appeared in the form of northers to break up meetings. James E. Ferguson reported on one of his revivals: "There was a heavy norther down upon us all the time of the meeting, and sin and cold so froze up the people's hearts that little good was done in comparison to some others."

At some churches the devil was accused of appearing in the form of a rat. Poles and split logs often served for construction timbers of meeting places. Cracks, both on the walls and roofs, were usually filled with grass and mud. This combination kept wind, rain, and cold out as long as it remained reasonably dry. But a dirt section of such structures always seemed to pose a gleeful challenge to any adventurous rat. When one dug a hole large enough to pass through on a roof, the rain in short time would increase it into a major tunnel. A dirty stream of cold water pouring down a collar or into a lap was enough to try the patience of a saint.

Many of the big churches of the nation had notably humble beginnings. Their stories are legion. One example will suffice: For a long time the Baptists of Houston talked, without success, of establishing a church. Finally a bit of horseplay—muleplay, to be exact—turned the tide. Someone, as a joke, contributed a raw-boned mule to start a building fund. But instead of being offended, the hopeful Baptists fattened the lean mule and sold it. And then with a nucleus for a building fund, they were encouraged to hold a fair at which they sold useful homemade articles. The fattened mule and the fair brought them $450.[23] Thus, beginning with a poor mule that nobody wanted, and faith that everybody needed, the Houston Baptists never wavered until the First Baptist Church was a reality.

From such humble starts, whether a contribution in the amount of a poor mule or a widow's mite, religious momentum picked up on the struggling frontier and never stopped until church steeples pointing upward from all over concrete cities and green countrysides came to symbolize a land of believers, and an established way of life.

NOTES

Chapter 1

1. See Herbert Asbury, *A Methodist Saint* (New York: Alfred A. Knopf, Inc., 1927), p. 117.

2. These statistics are based on Archie Robertson, *That Old-Time Religion* (Boston: Houghton Mifflin Company, 1950), pp. 29, 53, 69, and William Warren Sweet, *The Story of Religions in America* (New York: Harper & Brothers, 1930, 1939), pp. 7–8.

3. For conditions, see further Stuart N. Lake, *Wyatt Earp, Frontier Marshal* (Boston and New York: Houghton Mifflin Company, 1931), p. 3.

4. New York: Charles Scribner's Sons, 1922, p. 84.

5. John Ervin Kirkpatrick, *Timothy Flint* (Cleveland: The Arthur H. Clark Company, 1911), p. 125.

6. Charles A. Johnson, *The Frontier Camp Meeting* (Dallas: © Southern Methodist University Press, 1955), p. 9.

7. Mody C. Boatright, *Folk Laughter on the American Frontier* (New York: The Macmillan Company, 1949), p. 134.

8. For other anecodotes about religious ignorance, see *Coyote Wisdom*, ed. J. Frank Dobie, Mody C. Boatright, Harry Ransom (Austin: Texas Folk-Lore Society, 1938), pp. 158–62.

9. Kirkpatrick, *op. cit.*, p. 102.

10. *A Treasury of American Anecdotes*, ed. B. A. Botkin (New York: Random House, 1957), pp. 123–24.

[11.] Macum Phelan, *A History of Early Methodism in Texas, 1817–1866* (Nashville: Cokesbury Press, 1924), p. 36.

[12.] For account of early Episcopal movement, see Du Bose Murphy, *A Short History of the Protestant Episcopal Church in Texas* (Dallas: Turner, 1935).

[13.] O. W. Nolan, "Sheriff When Nueces Was Dead," *Frontier Times* (Bandera, Texas, January 1932), p. 167.

[14.] From *Hands Up!* as told by Fred E. Sutton and written down by A. B. Macdonald, copyright 1926, 1927 by The Bobbs-Merrill Company, 1955, by A. B. Macdonald, reprinted by permission of the publishers.

[15.] *Ibid.*, pp. 148–49.

[16.] *Houston Morning Star*, June 18, 1839.

[17.] B. F. Riley, *History of the Baptists in Texas* (Dallas, 1907), p. 113. Privately published.

[18.] John William Rogers, *The Lusty Texans of Dallas* (New York: E. P. Dutton & Co., Inc., 1951), pp. 184–85.

[19.] Paul Crume, *Dallas Morning News*, March 12, 1953.

[20.] *Frontier Times* (Bandera, Texas, April 1948), p. 178.

[21.] Quoted in Noah Smithwick, *The Evolution of a State* (Austin: The Steck Company, 1900), p. 321.

Chapter II

[1.] *The Acts* 4:13.

[2.] Harold Preece and Celia Kraft, *Dew on Jordan,* quoted in *A Treasury of Southern Folklore,* ed. B. A. Botkin (New York: Crown Publishers, Inc., 1949), p. 94.

[3.] *Autobiography of Peter Cartwright, The Backwoods Preacher,* ed. W. P. Strickland (Cincinnati and New York: Carlton and Porter, 1857), p. 486.

[4.] Walter Brownlow Posey, *The Baptist Church in the Lower Mississippi Valley, 1776–1845* (Lexington: University of Kentucky Press, 1957), p. 21.

[5.] *Ibid.*, pp. 22–27.

6. *Ibid.*

7. Timothy Flint, *Recollection of the Last Ten Years* . . . (Boston: Cummings, Hilliard and Company, 1826), p. 64.

8. I. E. Gates, *Watching the World Go By* (Nashville: The Baptist Sunday School Board, 1930), p. 32.

9. New York: W. W. Norton & Company, Inc., 1940, p. 329.

10. William Warren Sweet, *Religion on the American Frontier:* Vol. IV, *The Methodists, 1783–1840* (Chicago: University of Chicago Press, 1946), p. 67.

11. "A Texas Preacher" (Nashville: Southern Methodist Publishing House, 1884), pp. 94–95.

12. Ellis M. Coulter, *William G. Brownlow, Fighting Parson of the Southern Highlands* (Chapel Hill: University of North Carolina Press, 1937), p. 9.

13. James D. Davis, *A History of the City of Memphis* (Memphis: Hite, Crumpton and Kelly, 1873), p. 219.

14. Coulter, *op. cit.,* p. 20.

15. "The Diary of a Frontier Preacher," *Frontier Times* (Bandera, Texas, August 1939), p. 500.

16. John Ervin Kirkpatrick, *Timothy Flint* (Cleveland: The Arthur H. Clark Company, 1911), p. 70.

17. Posey, *op. cit.,* p. 28.

18. *Ibid.,* pp. 28–29.

19. *Ibid.,* p. 23.

20. Kirkpatrick, *op. cit.,* p. 95.

21. *Ibid.,* pp. 107–8.

22. C. L. Sonnichsen in *Cowboys and Cattle Kings* (Norman: University of Oklahoma Press, 1950), p. 178, gives a version of this anecdote.

Chapter III

1. Noah Smithwick, *The Evolution of a State* (Austin: The Steck Company, 1900), p. 155.

[2] William Warren Sweet, *Religion on the American Frontier: Vol. I, The Baptists, 1783–1830* (Chicago: University of Chicago Press, 1931), p. 642.

[3] For further description of the frontier preacher and his ways, see Henry Fowler, *The American Pulpit* (New York, 1856), p. 130.

[4] "A Texas Preacher," *Five Years in the West* (Nashville: Southern Methodist Publishing House, 1884), pp. 103–4.

[5] Raymond W. Thorp, *Bowie Knife* (Albuquerque: The University of New Mexico Press, 1948), p. 62.

[6] Nashville: Broadman Press, 1937, p. 98.

[7] Archie Robertson, *That Old-Time Religion* (Boston: Houghton Mifflin Company, 1950), p. 47.

[8] John A. Lomax, "Adventures of a Ballad Hunter," in *From Hell to Breakfast*, ed. Mody C. Boatright and Donald Day (Austin: Texas Folk-Lore Society, 1944), p. 17.

[9] Boyce House, *Roundup of Texas Humor* (San Antonio: The Naylor Company, 1943), p. 44. Also personal recollection.

[10] Donald Day, *Big Country: Texas* (New York: Duell Sloan & Pearce, Inc., 1947), pp. 61–62.

[11] Chris Emmett, *Shanghai Pierce* (Norman: University of Oklahoma Press, 1953), p. 173.

[12] *Ibid.*, p. 8.

[13] Mody C. Boatright, *Folk Laughter on the American Frontier* (New York: The Macmillan Company, 1949), p. 142.

[14] *A Treasury of Western Folklore*, ed. B. A. Botkin (New York: Crown Publishers, Inc., 1951), p. 88.

[15] *A Treasury of American Anecdotes*, ed. B. A. Botkin (New York: Random House, 1957), p. 121.

[16] Owen P. White, *Lead and Likker* (New York: Minton, Balch & Company, 1932), p. 273.

[17] *A Treasury of Southern Folklore*, ed. B. A. Botkin (New York: Crown Publishers, Inc., 1949), p. 103.

[18] Told by Boyce House, *op. cit.*, p. 36.

[19] *Ibid.*, p. 93.

[20] J. B. Cranfill, *Chronicles* (Nashville: Broadman Press, 1937), p. 98.

[21] B. A. Botkin, *A Treasury of American Anecdotes*, p. 123.

[22] Walter Brownlow Posey, *The Baptist Church in the Lower Mississippi Valley, 1776–1845* (Lexington: University of Kentucky Press, 1957), p. 16.

[23] J. Evetts Haley, *Charles Goodnight* (Norman: University of Oklahoma Press, 1949), p. 187.

[24] *Ibid.*, p. 186.

[25] Shine Philips, *Big Spring* (New York: Prentice-Hall, Inc., 1945), p. 49.

[26] For excellent first-hand account of Spanish laws and their effect on marriage, see Smithwick, *op. cit.*, pp. 66–67.

[27] Marjorie Rogers, "Morrell, the Pioneer Preacher," *Frontier Times* (Bandera, Texas, March 1932), p. 261.

[28] Stanley Vestal, *Short Grass Country* (New York: Duell, Sloan & Pearce, Inc., 1941), pp. 103–4.

[29] Roselle Williams Crawford, *Survival of Legends* (San Antonio: The Naylor Company, 1952), p. 24.

[30] Requoted in *Frontier Times* (December 1947), p. 70.

[31] J. B. Cranfill and J. L. Walker, *R. C. Buckner's Life of Faith and Works* (Dallas: Buckner Orphans Home, 1916), p. 244.

[32] Robertson, *op. cit.*, p. 259.

[33] For account of early Texas marriage and divorce, see Bascom Giles and Curtis Bishop, *Lots of Land* (Austin: The Steck Company, 1949), pp. 37–38.

[34] Crawford, *op. cit.*, pp. 23–24.

[35] Ruel McDaniel, *Vinegarroon* (Kingsport: Southern Publishers, 1936), pp. 136–37. C. L. Sonnichsen, *Roy Bean* (New York: The Macmillan Company, 1943), p. 115.

[36] Sonnichsen, *Op cit.*, p. 117.

37. Crawford, *op. cit.*, p. 24.

38. Quoted by Jim Feagin, *Fifty Years under the Bench in Texas* (San Antonio: The Naylor Company, 1950), pp. 64–65. Used by permission.

Chapter IV

1. Henry Fowler, *The American Pulpit* (New York, 1856), p. 130.

2. The original publisher of this sermon is not known. The *Frontier Times* (Bandera, Texas, May 1939), pp. 349–51, has printed it. The editor quoted a letter from W. A. Briggs of Harlington, Texas, stating that he had had a clipping of the sermon for over forty years, and "I don't think there is any question but what it was delivered." Published courtesy of *Frontier Times* magazine.

3. New York: George H. Doran Company, 1910, pp. 60–64.

4. Charles A. Johnson, *The Frontier Camp Meeting* (Dallas: © Southern Methodist University Press, 1955), p. 116.

5. John A. Lomax, *Adventures of a Ballad Hunter* (New York: The Macmillan Company, 1947), pp. 224–26. Lomax did some splendid and valuable tape recordings, particularly among the Negroes. Used by special permission.

6. See account by J. B. Cranfill in *Chronicles* (Nashville: Broadman Press, 1937), p. 315. For fuller account of McDonald, see Albert Bigelow Paine, *Captain Bill McDonald, Texas Ranger* (New York: J. J. Little & Ives Company, 1909).

7. Quoted by Mody C. Boatright in *Backwoods to Border*, ed. Mody C. Boatright and Donald Day (Dallas: Texas Folk-Lore Society, 1943), p. 77.

Chapter V

1. Quoted in Macum Phelan, *A History of the Expansion of Methodism in Texas, 1867–1902* (Dallas: Mathis, Van Nort & Company, 1937), p. 173.

2. Dallas: Cokesbury Press, 1924, p. 315.

8. See Charles A. Johnson, *The Frontier Camp Meeting* (Dallas: © Southern Methodist University Press, 1955), pp. 188–89.

4. M. Emory Wright, quoted in Johnson, *Ibid.*, p. 188.

5. *Ibid.*

6. William Warren Sweet, *Religion on the American Frontier: Vol. I, The Baptists, 1783–1830* (Chicago: University of Chicago Press, 1931), p. 272.

7. John Ervin Kirkpatrick, *Timothy Flint* (Cleveland: The Arthur H. Clark Company, 1911), p. 69.

8. *Ibid.*, p. 67.

9. Johnson, *op. cit.*, p. 190.

10. *Baptist Banner and Pioneer*, Louisville, August 20, 1840. Johnson, *op. cit.*, p. 189.

11. See *A Treasury of American Anecdotes*, ed. B. A. Botkin (New York: Random House, 1957), p. 11.

12. Quoted in Macum Phelan, *A History of Early Methodism in Texas, 1817–1866* (Nashville: Cokesbury Press, 1924), p. 469.

13. *Ibid.*

14. Goose Creek, Texas: J. W. Anderson & Sons, 1907, p. 95.

15. A version of this story is related by Archie Robertson, *That Old-Time Religion* (Boston: Houghton Mifflin Company, 1950), p. 19.

16. *Ibid.*, p. 80.

17. *Following General Sam Houston* (Austin: The Steck Company, 1935), p. 154.

18. Jesse L. Boyd, *A History of the Baptists in America Prior to 1845* (New York: American Press, 1957), p. 74.

19. Nashville: Baptist Sunday School Board, 1930, p. 102.

Chapter VI

1. S. O. Young, *A Thumb-nail History of the City of Houston* (Houston: Press of Rein & Sons Company, 1912), pp. 109–10. Macum Phelan, *A History of Early Methodism in Texas, 1817–1866* (Nashville: Cokesbury Press, 1924), pp. 79–80.

2. Dallas: Smith & Lamar, 1912, p. 383.

[3.] Phelan, *op. cit.*, p. 79.

[4.] *Watchman of the South*, June 11, 1840, quoted in Jesse Guy Smith, *Heroes of the Saddle Bags* (San Antonio: The Naylor Company, 1951), p. 15.

[5.] J. W. Anderson, *From the Plains to the Pulpit* (Goose Creek, Texas: J. W. Anderson & Sons, 1907), pp. 276–78.

[6.] Macum Phelan, *A History of the Expansion of Methodism in Texas, 1867–1902* (Dallas: Mathis, Van Nort & Company, 1937), pp. 267–68.

[7.] J. Evetts Haley, *Charles Goodnight* (Norman: University of Oklahoma Press, 1949), p. 105.

[8.] New York: Harper & Brothers, 1952, p. 60.

[9.] Jesse Guy Smith, *op. cit.*, p. 87.

[10.] For account of Murrell, see Ross Phares, *Reverend Devil, A Biography of John A. Murrell* (New Orleans: Pelican Publishing Company, 1941).

Chapter VII

[1.] John Rippon, *Baptist Annual Register for 1801 and 1802* in Walter Brownlow Posey, *The Baptist Church in the Lower Mississippi Valley, 1776–1845* (Lexington: University of Kentucky Press, 1957), p. 55.

[2.] William Warren Sweet, *Religion on the American Frontier: Vol. I, The Baptists, 1783–1830* (Chicago: University of Chicago Press, 1931), pp. 136–37.

[3.] J. M. Keating, *History of the City of Memphis and Shelby County, Tennessee* (Syracuse: D. Mason & Company, 1888, 3 vols.), p. 153.

[4.] *Plantation and Frontier Documents*, ed. Ulrich B. Phillips (Cleveland: The Arthur H. Clark Company, 1909), Vol. VII, pp. 284–86.

[5.] Sweet, *op. cit.*, p. 10.

[6.] *Autobiography of Reverend James B. Finley*, ed. W. P. Strickland (Cincinnati: Cranston and Curts, 1853), p. 167.

7. Jesse L. Boyd, *A History of the Baptists in America Prior to 1845* (New York: American Press, 1957), p. 77.

8. Sweet, *op. cit.*, p. 11.

9. From Charles A. Johnson, *The Frontier Camp Meeting* (Dallas: © Southern Methodist University Press, 1955), p. 141.

10. John Trotwood Moore and Austin P. Foster, *Tennessee, the Volunteer State, 1769–1923* (Chicago and Nashville: The S. J. Clark Publishing Company, 1923), p. 332.

11. Ellis M. Coulter, *William G. Brownlow, Fighting Parson of the Southern Highlands* (Chapel Hill: University of North Carolina Press, 1937), p. 11.

12. *Autobiography of Peter Cartwright, The Backwoods Preacher*, ed. W. P. Strickland (Cincinnati and New York: Carlton and Porter, 1857), p. 11.

13. Moore and Foster, *loc. cit.*

14. Timothy Flint, *Recollections of the Last Ten Years* . . . (Boston: Cummings, Hilliard and Company, 1826), p. 365.

15. Letter of George Baxter, quoted in Johnson, *op. cit.*, p. 58.

16. *Autobiography of Peter Cartwright, The Backwoods Preacher*, *op. cit.*, pp. 51–52.

17. *Ibid.*, p. 87.

18. Moore and Foster, *loc. cit.*

19. Coulter, *op. cit.*, p. 12.

20. Keating, *loc. cit.*

21. *Ibid.*

22. Quoted in Ernest Sutherland Bates, *American Faith* (New York: W. W. Norton & Co., Inc., 1940), p. 339.

23. Baxter, *loc. cit.*

24. In Johnson, *op. cit.*, p. 54.

25. Bates, *op. cit.*, p. 339.

26. *Ibid.*, p. 338.

27. See Johnson, *op. cit.*, p. 211.

28. Moore and Foster, *loc. cit.*

29. For further evaluation from this angle, see Bates, *op. cit.*, p. 340.

Chapter VIII

1. Walter Brownlow Posey, *The Baptist Church in the Lower Mississippi Valley, 1776–1845* (Lexington: University of Kentucky Press, 1957), p. 39.

2. *Ibid.*, p. 44. William Warren Sweet, *Religion on the American Frontier: Vol. I, The Baptists, 1783–1830* (Chicago: University of Chicago Press, 1931), p. 367.

3. Sweet, *op. cit.*, p. 50.

4. *Ibid.*, p. 379.

5. Posey, *op. cit.*, p. 50.

6. See William Warren Sweet, *Religion in the Development of American Culture, 1765–1840* (New York: Charles Scribner's Sons, 1952), p. 140.

7. Sweet, *The Baptist*, p. 379.

8. In his *Autobiography*, Cartwright makes numerous favorable references to the use of liquor.

9. In his *Autobiography*, Finley makes various references to liquor.

10. Archie Robertson, *That Old-Time Religion* (Boston: Houghton Mifflin Company, 1950), p. 72.

11. John James, *My Experience with Indians* (Austin: Gammel's Book Store, 1925), p. 41.

12. *Galveston News Anecdote Contest* (Galveston, 1902), in Mody C. Boatright, *Folk Laughter on the American Frontier* (New York: The Macmillan Company, 1949), p. 143.

13. Robertson, *op. cit.*, p. 73.

14. See Sweet, *The Baptists*, for reproduced church minutes showing numerous such examples.

15. J. M. Carroll, *History of the Texas Baptists* (Dallas: Baptist Standard Publishing Company, 1923), p. 125.

16. Shine Philips, *Big Spring* (New York: Prentice-Hall, Inc., 1945), p. 79.

17. "A Texas Preacher," *Five Years in the West* (Nashville: Southern Methodist Publishing House, 1884), pp. 127–30.

18. Posey, *op. cit.*, p. 45.

19. Sweet, *The Baptists*, p. 285.

20. *Ibid.*, pp. 289, 311.

21. *Ibid.*, pp. 270–71.

22. *Ibid.*, p. 250.

23. Will N. Calhoun, "A Few of Quantrill's Men in Texas," *Frontier Times* (Bandera, Texas, June 1946), pp. 169–70. Published courtesy of *Frontier Times* magazine.

24. Posey, *op. cit.*, pp. 44–45.

25. James J. Burnett, *Sketches of Tennessee's Pioneer Baptist Preachers* (Jefferson City, Tennessee: Privately published, 1919), pp. 561–62.

26. A. W. Eddins, "Anecdotes from the Brazos Bottoms," *Straight Texas*, ed. J. Frank Dobie and Mody C. Boatright (Austin: Texas Folk-Lore Society, 1937), pp. 93–94.

27. For further accounts of uses of tobacco on the frontier, see Noah Smithwick, *The Evolution of a State* (Austin: The Steck Company, 1900), pp. 18, 53, 143, 182, 330.

28. Bascom Giles and Curtis Bishop, *Lots of Land* (Austin: The Steck Company, 1949), p. 199.

29. Jim Feagin, *Fifty Years under the Bench in Texas* (San Antonio: The Naylor Company, 1950), p. 103.

30. Owen P. White, *My Texas 'Tis of Thee* (New York: G. P. Putnam's Sons, 1936), p. 252.

31. Curtis Bishop, "This Day in Texas," *San Angelo Standard-Times* (San Angelo, Texas, September 20, 1948).

32. "Records of the Forks of Elkhorn Baptist Church, Kentucky, 1800–1820," in Sweet, *The Baptists*, pp. 272–416.

33. James Leaton, *History of Methodism in Illinois, from 1793 to 1832* (Cincinnati, 1883), p. 387.

[34] "When Sam Jones Came to Texas," *Frontier Times* (Bandera, Texas, November 1931), p. 53.

[35] Mabelle Purcell, *Two Texas Female Seminaries* (Wichita Falls: Texas University Press, Midwestern University, 1951), pp. 165–66.

[36] William Warren Sweet, *Religion on the American Frontier: Vol. II, The Presbyterians, 1783–1840* (Chicago: The University of Chicago Press, 1936), p. 66.

[37] Ebenezer Church Minutes, *Ibid.*, pp. 251–57.

[38] Sweet, *Ibid.*, p. 255.

[39] Macum Phelan, *A History of Early Methodism in Texas, 1817–1866* (Nashville: Cokesbury Press, 1924), p. 41.

[40] William Warren Sweet, *Religion on the American Frontier: Vol. IV, The Methodists, 1783–1840* (Chicago: University of Chicago Press, 1946), p. 672.

Chapter IX

[1] Austin to Seguin, *The Austin Papers*, ed. Eugene C. Barker (Washington: Government Printing Office, Vols. I and II; Austin: University of Texas, Vol. III, 1924, 1927, 1928), Vol. I, p. 718.

[2] *Ibid.*, Vol. I, p. 172.

[3] Austin to Josiah Bell, February 24, 1829. *Ibid.*, Vol. II, p. 173.

[4] William Stuart Red, *The Texas Colonists and Religion, 1821–1836* (Austin: E. L. Shettles, 1924), p. 75.

[5] Recollections of the author.

[6] See William R. Hogan, *The Texas Republic* (Norman: University of Oklahoma Press, 1946), p. 195.

[7] *Autobiography of Peter Cartwright, The Backwoods Preacher*, ed. W. P. Strickland (Cincinnati and New York: Carlton and Porter, 1857), p. 121.

[8] *A Journey through Texas* (New York: Dix Edwards and Company, 1857), p. 77.

[9] See William Warren Sweet, *Religion on the American Frontier: Vol. I, The Baptists, 1783–1830* (Chicago: University of Chicago Press, 1931), p. 12.

10. Quoted in Macum Phelan, *A History of Early Methodism in Texas, 1817–1866* (Nashville: Cokesbury Press, 1924), p. 388.

11. Hogan, *op. cit.*, p. 194.

12. *Ibid.*, p. 119.

13. Strickland, *op. cit.*, pp. 32, 134.

14. Hogan, *op. cit.*, p. 204.

15. In Phelan, *op. cit.*, p. 327.

16. I. E. Gates, *Watching the World Go By* (Nashville: The Baptist Sunday School Board, 1930), p. 170.

17. *Ibid.*, p. 26.

18. *The Book of Negro Folklore*, ed. Langston Hughes and Arna Bontemps (New York: Dodd, Mead & Co., 1958), p. 158.

19. Gates, *op. cit.*, p. 163.

20. Macum Phelan, *A History of the Expansion of Methodism in Texas, 1867–1902* (Dallas: Mathis, Van Nort & Company, 1937), p. 21.

21. William Warren Sweet, *Religion on the American Frontier: Vol. II, The Presbyterians, 1783–1840* (Chicago: University of Chicago Press, 1936), p. 21.

22. Gates, *op. cit.*, p. 165.

23. Archie Robertson, *That Old-Time Religion* (Boston: Houghton Mifflin Company, 1950), pp. 120, 228. And personal recollections of the author.

24. Macum Phelan, *A History of Early Methodism in Texas, 1817–1866*, p. 328.

25. *Ibid.*, p. 349.

26. Strickland, *op. cit.*, p. 357.

27. *A Treasury of Southern Folklore*, ed. B. A. Botkin (New York: Crown Publishers, 1949), p. 95.

28. New York: Minton, Balch & Company, 1932, p. 98.

29. Quoted in Boyce House, *Roundup of Texas Humor* (San Antonio: The Naylor Company, 1943), p. 197.

[80] Robertson, *op. cit.*, p. 80. And personal recollections of the author.

Chapter X

[1] Address of Charles F. Colcord, a buffalo hunter who became a leading pioneer and industrialist of Oklahoma, in Stanley Vestal, *Short Grass Country* (New York: Duell, Sloan & Pearce, Inc., 1941), pp. 104–7.

[2] Macum Phelan, *A History of the Expansion of Methodism in Texas, 1867–1902* (Dallas: Mathis, Van Nort & Company, 1937), p. 22.

[3] *Ibid.*, p. 340.

[4] J. B. Cranfill, *Chronicles* (Nashville: Broadman Press, 1937), p. 120.

[5] Duncan W. Robinson, *Texas' Three-Legged Willie* (Austin: Texas State Historical Association, 1948), preface p. 5.

[6] *A Treasury of Southern Folklore*, ed. B. A. Botkin (New York: Crown Publishers, 1949), p. 97.

[7] Stanley Vestal, *Queen of Cowtowns, Dodge City* (New York: Harper & Brothers, 1952), pp. 3–4.

[8] Mrs. W. L. Williams, *Golden Years, An Autobiography* (Dallas: Baptist Standard Publishing Company, 1921), p. 76.

[9] William MacLeod Raine, *Guns of the Frontier* (New York: World Publishing Company, 1940), p. 110.

[10] Mody C. Boatright, *Folk Laughter on the American Frontier* (New York: The Macmillan Company, 1949), p. 136.

[11] Excerpt from *The Red-Blooded Heroes of the Frontier* by Edgar Beecher Bronson, reprinted by permission of Brandt & Brandt.

[12] A slightly varied version is carried in Boyce House, *Roundup of Texas Humor* (San Antonio: The Naylor Company, 1943), p. 155.

[13] *Straight Texas*, ed. J. Frank Dobie and Mody C. Boatright (Austin: Texas Folk-Lore Society, 1937), p. 97.

[14] James Ross, *Life and Times of Rueben Ross* (Philadelphia, 1888), p. 208.

[15] *Straight Texas*, pp. 98–99.

Chapter XI

[1.] Macum Phelan, *A History of the Expansion of Methodism in Texas, 1867–1902* (Dallas: Mathis, Van Nort & Company, 1937), p. 174.

[2.] *Autobiography of Peter Cartwright, The Backwoods Preacher*, ed. W. P. Strickland (Cincinnati and New York: Carlton and Porter, 1857), pp. 323, 353–54.

[3.] *A Treasury of American Anecdotes*, ed. B. A. Botkin (New York: Random House, 1957), p. 129.

[4.] Phelan, *op. cit.*, pp. 356–57.

[5.] *Ibid.*, pp. 128–29.

[6.] *Butterfield 7 Years with the Wild Indians* (O'Donnell, Texas, 1945), p. 34. Privately published by Ben Moore, Sr.

[7.] Will N. Calhoun, "A Few of Quantrill's Men in Texas," *Frontier Times* (Bandera, Texas, June 1946), p. 169. Published courtesy of *Frontier Times* magazine.

[8.] John Myers Myers, *The Alamo* (New York: E. P. Dutton & Co., Inc., 1948), p. 100.

[9.] See Josephine Polley Golson, *Bailey's Light* (San Antonio: The Naylor Company, 1950), p. 53.

[10.] See *Hands Up!* as told by Fred E. Sutton and written down by A. B. Macdonald, copyright 1926, 1927 by The Bobbs-Merrill Company, 1955 by A. B. Macdonald, pp. 29–30.

[11.] John William Rogers, *The Lusty Texans of Dallas* (New York: E. P. Dutton & Co., Inc., 1951), pp. 145–46.

Chapter XII

[1.] William Warren Sweet, *Religion on the American Frontier: Vol. I, The Baptists, 1783–1830* (Chicago: University of Chicago Press, 1931), p. 21.

[2.] *Autobiography of Peter Cartwright, The Backwoods Preacher*, ed. W. P. Strickland (Cincinnati and New York: Carlton and Porter, 1857), p. 486.

[3.] Quoted in Macum Phelan, *A History of the Expansion of Methodism in Texas, 1867–1902* (Dallas: Mathis, Van Nort & Company, 1937), p. 22.

4. From Charles A. Johnson, *The Frontier Camp Meeting* (Dallas: © Southern Methodist University Press, 1955), p. 159.

5. Quoted in J. B. Cranfill and J. L. Walker, *R. C. Buckner's Life of Faith and Works* (Dallas: Buckner Orphans Home, 1916), p. 9.

6. Francis Asbury, *Journal*, Vol. III, quoted in Johnson, *op. cit.*, p. 156.

7. "The Diary of a Frontier Preacher," *Frontier Times* (Bandera, Texas, August 1939), p. 499.

8. Peter W. Gravis, *Twenty-Five Years on the Outside Row* in Phelan, *op. cit.*, p. 20.

9. *Frontier Times* (Bandera, Texas, November 1946), p. 269.

10. Cranfill and Walker, *op. cit.*, p. 44.

11. "Preachers and Teachers" in *This Is the West*, ed. R. W. Howard (New York: The New American Library, 1957), p. 128.

12. W. A. Young, "Early Days in the Ministry," *Frontier Times* (Bandera, Texas, February 1946), p. 78.

13. Phelan, *op. cit.*, p. 66.

14. *Ibid.*, p. 42.

15. *Ibid.*, p. 248.

16. Sweet, *op. cit.*, p. 68.

17. *A Treasury of American Anecdotes*, ed. B. A. Botkin (New York: Random House, 1957), p. 114.

18. Herbert Asbury, *The Barbary Coast* (New York: Garden City Publishing Company, 1933), pp. 115–17.

19. Marshall, Texas, 1920, p. 182.

20. Phelan, *op. cit.*, pp. 139–40.

21. *Ibid.*, p. 83.

22. B. F. Riley, *History of the Baptists in Texas* (Dallas, 1907), p. 112.

23. S. O. Young, *A Thumb-nail History of the City of Houston* (Houston, 1912), p. 114.